WB 18.2 FAR £17.99

Essential Statistics for Medical Examinations

Second Edition

Essential Statistics for Medical Examinations

Second Edition

E Brian Faragher PhD FSS
Senior Lecturer in Medical Statistics
Liverpool School of Tropical Medicine
Liverpool

MONKLANDS HOSPITAL
LIBRARY
MONKSCOURT AVENUE
AIRDRIE ML60JS
☎01236712005

© 2005 PASTEST LTD
Egerton Court
Parkgate Estate
Knutsford
Cheshire
WA16 8DX

Telephone: 01565 752000

All rights reserved. No part of this publication may be reproduced, stored in a retrieval system, or transmitted, in any form or by any means, electronic, mechanical, photocopying, recording or otherwise without the prior permission of the copyright owner.

PasTest would like to thank the following authors for their contribution to our online product from which limited text is taken for use in this title: P. Ambery, K. Binymin, D. Namison, K. Prescott and Ranjan

First Published 1998
Second Edition 2005

ISBN: 1 904627 633

A catalogue record for this book is available from the British Library.

The information contained within this book was obtained by the author from reliable sources. However, while every effort has been make to ensure its accuracy, no responsibility for loss, damage or injury occasioned to any person acting or refraining from action as a result of information contained herein can be accepted by the publishers or author.

PasTest Revision Books and Intensive Courses

PasTest has been established in the field of postgraduate medical education since 1972, providing revision books and intensive study courses for doctors preparing for their professional examinations. Books and courses are available for the following specialties:

MRCGP, MRCP Parts 1 and 2, MRCPCH Parts 1 and 2, MRCPsych, MRCS, MRCOG Parts 1 and 2, DRCOG, DCH, FRCA, PLAB Parts 1 and 2.

For further details contact:

PasTest, Freepost, Knutsford, Cheshire WA16 7BR
Tel: 01565 752000 Fax: 01565 650264
Email: enquiries@pastest.co.uk Web site: www.pastest.co.uk

Text prepared by Vision Typesetting Ltd, Manchester
Printed and bound in the UK by Athenaeum Press Limited, Gateshead

Contents

Recommended reading list ix
Preface xi

1 Basic concepts and definitions **1**
1.1 Why are statistics necessary? 1
1.2 Populations and samples 2
1.3 Sources of variation/error 4
1.3.1 Measurement error 4
1.3.2 Within-individual (natural) variation 5
1.3.3 Between-individuals variation 5
1.3.4 Systematic effects 6
1.3.5 Sample variation/error 6
1.3.6 Unknown/unobserved variation 7
1.4 Study design principles 8

2 Measurements **10**
2.1 Types of data 10
2.1.1 Qualitative measures 10
2.1.2 Quantitative measures 11
2.2 Accuracy and precision 12
2.3 Validity 13

3 Probability **14**
3.1 Definitions 14
3.2 Properties of probability 15
3.2.1 Mutually exclusive categories 16
3.2.2 Independent events 17
3.3 Sensitivity and specificity 17

4 Important distributions **20**
4.1 What is a distribution? 20
4.2 Binomial distribution 20
4.3 Poisson distribution 23

4.4 Normal (Gaussian) distribution 23
4.5 Standard Normal distribution 26
4.6 Student *t*-distribution 27
4.7 Non-Normal (continuous) distributions 27
4.8 Log-Normal (continuous) distributions 29
4.9 Normalising transformations 29

5 Basic descriptive statistics 32
5.1 Importance of descriptive statistics 32
5.2 Descriptive statistics for qualitative/categorical data 33
5.2.1 Odds ratios/relative incidence ratios 35
5.3 Descriptive statistics for quantitative data 35
5.3.1 Measures of central tendency 36
5.3.2 Measures of dispersion (variation): Normally distributed observations 38
5.3.3 Measures of dispersion (variation): non-Normally distributed observations 41
5.3.4 Quantiles 41
5.3.5 Effect size 43

6 Graphical presentation of data 44
6.1 Qualitative measures 44
6.2 Quantitative data 45

7 Computing confidence intervals 50
7.1 General concept 50
7.2 Standard errors 51
7.2.1 Quantitative data 51
7.2.2 Qualitative data 53
7.3 Computing confidence intervals 54
7.3.1 Confidence intervals for a Normal distribution (quantitative data) 54
7.3.2 Confidence intervals for a binomial distribution (qualitative data) 57
7.4 Reference ranges 58

8 Significance tests 59
8.1 Basic principles 59
8.2 Hypotheses and *P*-values 60
8.3 *P*-values 61
8.4 Type I and type II errors 62

8.5 Clinical vs statistical significance 63
8.6 Sample size and statistical power 64
8.7 General form of test statistics 65
8.8 Significance tests for qualitative data 66
8.8.1 Single sample 66
8.8.2 Two or more independent samples 67
8.8.3 Dependent samples 70
8.8.4 Number needed to treat 70
8.8.5 Worked example 71
8.9 Significance tests for quantitative (continuous) data 73
8.9.1 Parametric and non-parametric methods 73
8.9.2 Single samples 74
8.9.3 Two independent samples 74
8.9.4 Two dependent samples 76
8.9.5 More than two samples 77
8.10 Summary 78

9 Significance tests or confidence Intervals 79

10 Measures of association 82
10.1 Scatterplots 82
10.2 Correlation 83
10.2.1 Pearson correlation coefficient 87
10.2.2 Spearman correlation coefficient 87
10.2.3 Complex non-linear relationships 88
10.2.4 Confidence limits/significance tests for correlations 89
10.3 Linear regression 90
10.4 Logistic regression 92
10.5 Survival curves/Cox regression 93

11 Epidemiology – observational studies 95
11.1 Observational studies 95
11.1.1 Cross-sectional (prevalence) surveys 96
11.1.2 Cohort studies 99
11.1.3 Case–control studies 102
11.2 Association and causality 105

12 Interventional studies/clinical trials 108
12.1 Rationale for RCTs 108
12.2 Equipoise 110
12.3 Study protocols 110

12.3.1 Objectives 110
12.3.2 Design 111
12.3.3 Blinding of assessments 112
12.3.4 Inclusion/exclusion criteria 114
12.3.5 Interventions/treatments 115
12.3.6 Measurements 116
12.3.7 Allocation to treatment 116
12.3.8 Power/sample size 119
12.3.9 Statistical analysis plan 120
12.3.10 Informed consent 122
12.3.11 Research ethics committees 122
12.3.12 Dissemination of findings 123
12.4 Meta-analysis 123

13 Outline for critiquing a medical report 125

14 Sample best of five questions 127

Index 144

Recommended reading list

In the opinion of the authors, the definitive textbook on medical statistics is undoubtedly:

Practical Statistics for Medical Research: Altman D G, Chapman & Hall / CRC, 2006.

Given the huge importance now being given to the use of confidence intervals, particularly in the presentation of the results of randomised controlled trials, the following is also essential reading:

Statistics with Confidence: Gardner M J, Altman D G, Altman D (editor), Bryant T (editor), Gardner M (editor), Machin D (editor), BMJ Books, 2000.

For an excellent overview of epidemiological methods:

Epidemiological Studies: A Practical Guide: Silman A J, McFarlane G J (editor), Cambridge University Press, 2002.

Other highly recommended texts are:

An Introduction to Medical Statistics: Bland M, Oxford University Press, 2000.
Clinical Trials: A Practical Approach: Pocock S J, Wiley, 1996.
Essential Medical Statistics: Kirkwood B, Sterne J, Blackwell Science (UK), 2003.
How to Read a Paper: The Basics of Evidence Based Medicine: Greenhalgh T, BMJ Books, 2000.
Medical Statistics at a Glance: Petrie A, Sabin C, Blackwell Publishing, 2005.
Sample Size Tables for Clinical Studies (with disk): Machin D, Campbell M J, Fayers P M, Pinol A, Blackwell Science (UK), 1997.
Statistics at Square One: Swinscow T D V, Campbell M J (editor), BMJ Books, 2002.

Preface

As for the previous edition of this book, the primary purpose is to help candidates to prepare for medical examinations. The material included, therefore, covers the statistical design and analysis topics commonly chosen by medical examiners.

A previous knowledge of statistics is not assumed. Statistics is a branch of mathematics, so some mathematical content is inevitable – but this has been kept to a minimum. Emphasis is given instead to the basic concepts underlying statistical methods. Formulae have been included only where it is felt that these might help readers to understand a particular concept.

While this is not intended as a "statistical cookbook", an attempt has been made to indicate as clearly as possible the situations in which a particular method should be used, along with the assumptions the method requires (i.e. its limitations). However, readers should be aware that statistics is not an exact science. There is often more than one way of analysing a set of observations – and the choice of method can be quite subjective.

While this is quite a bit larger than the previous edition, it is still not a substitute for a good textbook on medical statistics. The extra length is due to the inclusion of more material than before. Some additional explanatory material has also been added to help with the understanding of the important basic concepts. Readers planning to apply statistical methods to real data are urged to acquire one of the many excellent textbooks already available – a recommended list of these is included in the reading list on page ix.

A set of multiple choice questions similar to those set by the Royal College Examination Boards is provided at the end of this book.

The author and publisher would also like to acknowledge the work of Chris Marguerie, co-author of the first edition.

1 Basic concepts and definitions

1.1 Why are statistics necessary?

THE RESULTS OBTAINED FROM CLINICAL TRIALS/ SURVEYS ARE OFTEN WRONG!

Data obtained from studies involving human beings (or, indeed, any biological system) vary, often considerably. There are many reasons for this, including:

- Studies are usually done on samples – these rarely (if ever) have exactly the same characteristics as the population they are taken from.
- Observations are rarely exact – some error is usually involved when a measurement is taken.
- Biological systems often fluctuate naturally, even when they appear to be in a steady state.
- There may be external influences (both random and systematic) acting on the observations.

A simple listing of the data obtained in a clinical study is unlikely to show any obvious patterns – the variation will conceal the real results. In addition, the chances are that the variation will also make the findings of the study inaccurate and imprecise – so drawing correct and sensible conclusions may prove to be difficult.

The effects of measurement error/variation cannot be removed completely, but good practice can help to reduce them. A good study design will help to limit and control the **known** sources of variation in a set of observations. However, there may also be some **unknown** sources of variation. By definition, these cannot be controlled or accounted for. Consequently, there will be uncertainty in the conclusions drawn from even the best conducted experiment.

In a sense, Donald Rumsfeld (US Defence Secretary) got it right in 2003 when he made his now (in)famous statement during the Iraq War:

> as we know, there are known knowns – there are things we know we know. We also know there are known unknowns – that is to say we know there are some things we do not know. But there are also unknown unknowns – that is, there are things we do not know that we do not know.

A good statistical analysis will estimate the amount of variation due to each known source of error and will extract the information needed to interpret the results of the study. More importantly, it will indicate the level of confidence (certainty) that can be attached to these results.

STATISTICS IS:

THE *SCIENCE* OF MEASURING THE (KNOWN) SOURCES OF VARIATION PRESENT IN AN EXPERIMENT.

THE *ART* OF DRAWING CORRECT CONCLUSIONS FROM INACCURATE INFORMATION.

1.2 Populations and samples

Target population: all people with the disease/condition of interest to whom the conclusions of the study will be applied.

Study population: the people actually available and accessible for study – this is usually limited to the subgroup of people with the disease/condition of interest attending the clinics where the study is being conducted.

Ideally, a clinical trial or survey should be conducted on every person with the disease or condition of interest. This is rarely possible. While it might be feasible to test a new treatment on all known patients with a rare condition, involving all known people with raised blood pressure in a study of a new anti-hypertensive drug would clearly be impossible.

Instead, a sample of people is usually selected and studied. This is perfectly acceptable – provided that a **representative sample** is selected from all of the people in the population of interest. Otherwise, the results obtained from the study cannot easily be generalised. A representative sample:

- has (within reasonable limits) the same characteristics as the target clinical population – so accurately reflects the variations (both random and systematic) within that target population
- can usually be obtained by choosing a sufficiently large **random sample**.

A **simple random sample**:

- is selected in such a way that (in theory at least) every individual in the target population has an equal chance of being chosen
- is nearly always the most appropriate type of sample for a clinical trial
- is usually obtained in practice by taking all eligible individuals who present to the participating clinics during the period of the study (ie it is assumed that patients present themselves in a random order).

A **stratified random sample**:

- may sometimes be more appropriate for a medical survey or observational study
- is selected in such a way that different proportions of people are recruited from particular sub-groups in the target population.

Example

A study is being planned to investigate how the lifestyle problems encountered by people with a continent stoma vary with age. The researchers are most interested in the problems found by adolescents, but expect to find most stomas in older patients. If they are right, a simple random sample might not recruit sufficient adolescents to produce interpretable findings. They thus divide the target clinical population into age decade sub-groups (15–24, 25–34, etc.) and recruit equal-sized random samples from within each age sub-group

1.3 Sources of variation/error

MEASUREMENTS OBTAINED FROM BIOLOGICAL SYSTEMS ARE INHERENTLY VARIABLE.

The following simple experiments all involve possibly the most basic and frequently made clinical observation: diastolic blood pressure (DBP). In each experiment, the DBP readings are taken under identical conditions. As the experiments become more complex, an increasing number of factors influence the DBP readings obtained. These factors tend to make the readings more and more variable.

1.3.1 Measurement error

Experiment 1: a single DBP reading is taken from a healthy individual.

This DBP reading is likely to be inaccurate due to **measurement error**. The size of this error will depend largely on the instrument used. A standard mercury sphygmomanometer is usually read with a digit preference for 0 or 5, ie the reading is rounded to the nearest whole number ending in 0 or 5 (eg 75, 80, 85). So, the measurement error with this instrument could be as much as ± 2.5 mmHg.

An electronic sphygmomanometer may record DBP to the nearest whole number (eg 75, 76, 77, etc.). The measurement error with this instrument will be much smaller, at ± 0.5 mmHg.

The amount of measurement error that is acceptable often depends on why the reading is being taken. In most clinical situations, DBP is screened to simply check that it is 'normal', in which case, an accuracy of ± 2.5 mmHg will be fine. In a clinical trial testing a new anti-hypertensive drug, however, an accuracy of ± 0.5 mmHg (or even better) may be needed.

1.3.2 Within-individual (natural) variation

Experiment 2: several DBP readings are taken from the same healthy individual at regular intervals.

Observations taken from the same person under identical conditions are called **replicates**. As in experiment 1, each replicate reading will be prone to measurement error.

In common with many biological factors, DBP levels fluctuate slightly around the 'true' underlying level even when a person is resting and in a steady state. This fluctuation may have a regular rhythm, but just a few readings taken over a short period of time will be unable to measure this accurately. The replicates will appear to vary randomly. Because of random variation, the readings obtained in this experiment are likely to differ from one another, but probably not by very much. The observations will vary around the 'true' underlying DBP level for this person.

The average of several replicate readings is likely to be closer to the 'true' underlying DBP level than a single reading. The average can be expected to get ever closer to this 'true' level as the number of replicates taken increases.

The number of replicates needed often depends on why the readings are being taken. To decide whether a patient is hypertensive and needing treatment, two replicates may be sufficient. To obtain the accuracy needed for a clinical trial, at least three replicates may be needed.

1.3.3 Between-individuals variation

Experiment 3: A single DBP reading is taken from each of several healthy individuals.

Again, all of the readings will be prone to random variation/error. Now, each person in the study will have their own underlying 'true' DBP level. This 'true' level can be assumed to be constant for each person, but it will, of course, differ between people.

If the people recruited into the study are a random sample from the target clinical population, the differences between individuals are usually considered to be acting randomly.

Technically, of course, each person exerts a fixed, or **systematic**, influence on the DBP readings obtained. Differences between individuals are rarely of interest, however, particularly in clinical trials – so the assumption that these are a random influence is usually perfectly reasonable.

> Measurement error, within-individual variation and differences between individuals are usually combined together and referred to collectively as ***random variation***.

1.3.4 Systematic effects

Experiment 4: single DBP readings are taken from several different patients with hypertension. Some are taking a drug to reduce their blood pressure, but the rest are not.

Once again, all of the DBP readings will be affected by measurement error and by differences between individuals. If the drug is effective, the treated patients should (on average) have lower 'true' underlying DBP levels than the others. For the purpose of statistical analysis, the effect of the drug is assumed to be constant across patients, ie the drug exerts a fixed, or systematic, influence on the readings obtained.

> Differences between observations that are due to the effect of a known factor (such as the effect of a drug) are called ***systematic variation***. It is the size of this systematic variation that is usually of primary interest in clinical research.

1.3.5 Sample variation/error

As well as the variation between the study observations, there will be error (variation) due to the study sample itself. The people recruited in Experiment 4 were randomly selected patients known to have mild hypertension. If selected properly, the characteristics of this sample will be similar, but not exactly identical, to those of the target clinical population of patients with mild hypertension.

If several random samples were taken from the same target clinical population, each sample would have similar, but not exactly identical, characteristics.

> The differences between the characteristics of a random sample and those of the population from which it is drawn are known as **random sampling variation**.

1.3.6 Unknown/unobserved variation

The differences in the DBP readings obtained in the above experiments will be due to:

- random variation only in Experiments 1, 2 and 3
- a combination of random and systematic variation in Experiment 4.

In general, as the complexity of the study increases, the number of possible sources of variation also increases, and so the range of the observations obtained tends to increase. We would expect the range of DBP readings to be smallest in Experiment 1 and greatest in Experiment 4.

In reality, the sources of variation/error acting on the observations made are rarely, if ever, known in full. In addition to the known sources, there are likely to be additional factors influencing the study observations, both systematically and randomly. Some may be totally unsuspected. Others may be suspected but too difficult to assess. In either case, the effects of these factors cannot be accounted for, either in the study design or in the statistical analysis.

Suppose, for example, that in Experiment 4 some patients prescribed the anti-hypertensive drug decide to explore their condition and treatment on the Internet. On the basis of what they find, they make changes to their lifestyle that also helps to reduce their blood pressure. This does not happen in the patients who are not given the drug – most may feel that, as their condition does not require medication, life is just fine as it is.

If the researchers are unaware of this, the influence of the lifestyle changes in the treated group on DBP levels will be missed. Any difference in average DBP level found between the two groups will be due to a combination of the effect of the drug and lifestyle changes – but all of the difference will probably be attributed to the drug!

1.4 Study design principles

PROPER CONSIDERATION OF THE LIKELY SOURCES OF OBSERVATION VARIATION ARE VITALLY IMPORTANT WHEN AN EXPERIMENT IS BEING PLANNED.

As far as possible, all potential sources of variation should be identified and incorporated into the study design. For example, suppose that the sphygmomanometer used for the treated patients in Experiment 4 consistently measures 5 mmHg too high, whereas the machine used in the untreated group is calibrated correctly. This difference is a source of systematic variation which, if not detected, will lead to the effect of the drug being under-estimated (by, on average, 5 mmHg).

This problem is easily resolved by good study design. The problem can be eradicated entirely by using the same machine in both groups. Or it can be balanced out by measuring equal numbers of patients in both groups with each machine.

A poorly designed study will almost certainly produce unreliable, misleading – or even invalid – findings. The most commonly occurring design flaws include:

- **Sampling bias** – this occurs when an unrepresentative (non-random) sample of individuals is selected from the target population.
- **Inadequate power** – this occurs when the study is too small and/or the amount of (random and systematic) variation acting on the observations is under-estimated, so the study is not able to detect the 'real' effect of a therapy.
- **Confounding** – this occurs when the outcome of specific interest cannot be distinguished from the effects of other (possibly unmeasured) factors acting in the study. For example, in Experiment 4, if advice on lifestyle changes is given to all patients prescribed the drug but to none of the untreated patients, the effect

of the anti-hypertensive drug cannot be separated from the effects of the lifestyle advice.

A POOR OR INVALID STATISTICAL ANALYSIS CAN BE REPEATED USING CORRECT METHODS BUT NO AMOUNT OF DATA MANIPULATION CAN COMPENSATE FOR FLAWS IN THE STUDY DESIGN.

2 Measurements

2.1 Types of data

THE DATA (MEASURES/VARIABLES) RECORDED IN MOST CLINICAL STUDIES CAN BE DIVIDED INTO DIFFERENT TYPES. IT IS VITAL TO DISTINGUISH BETWEEN THESE TYPES, AS EACH REQUIRES THE USE OF SLIGHTLY DIFFERENT STATISTICAL METHODS.

2.1.1 Qualitative measures

Nominal categorical measures

Nominal measures are used to classify individuals into distinct groups (categories) that have no obvious numerical relationship (eg blood group, gender). In a sense, these are not data at all.

Arbitrary numbers are attached to each category to provide labels (usually solely to allow the information to be handled by statistical computer programs).

Because the numbers allocated to the categories are arbitrary, they can be changed. For example, gender is sometimes coded as:

0 = male   1 = female

If you do not like these codes, the following work just as well:

1 = female   2 = male

or even, if you really prefer:

5 = male   17 = female.

Ordinal categorical measures

Ordinal measures are usually used to determine the extent to which patients are experiencing signs/symptoms that are essentially subjective (eg pain severity, mood).

Ordinal measures use categories with an inherent ranking across them. So, the numbers used to label the categories need to reflect this ordering. For example:

pain severity: 0 = nil 1 = mild 2 = moderate 3 = severe

A common criticism of ordinal measures is that they infer that the distances between the categories are all equal. This is unlikely to be true. Provided the underlying ordering is properly reflected, non-consecutive numbers can be used if these are considered to represent better the distances between the categories. For example:

pain severity: 0 = nil 1 = mild 4 = moderate 7 = severe

2.1.2 Quantitative measures

Quantitative measures produce numbers on a **continuous/interval** scale. The distance between adjacent numbers is constant. The numbers, and any changes in them, are physically interpretable. Unlike categorical measures, the numbers cannot be changed.

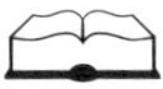

Example

A patient is found to have a haemoglobin level of 7.0 g/dl. This value will probably result in their receiving an appropriate drug treatment. Four weeks later, the value is 11.0 g/dl, in which case, the drug may be stopped or the dose reduced. In both instances, the numbers produced by the haemoglobin assay have a clear interpretation producing an appropriate clinical reaction.

Theoretically, most continuous measures can take any value within a specific range (eg weight, blood glucose, temperature). The actual values recorded depend on the measurement method and the precision required. So, for example, blood sodium and potassium levels have the same units, but whereas sodium is usually recorded to the nearest whole number (eg 141 mmol/l), potassium is usually recorded to one decimal place (eg 4.2 mmol/l).

Discrete continuous measures can only be whole numbers (integers). Such measures usually take the form of counts (eg number of asthma attacks suffered in the past four weeks).

2.2 Accuracy and precision

As described in Chapter 1, observations are prone to error. This is usually due to a combination of random and systematic factors. Two important elements of measurement error are **accuracy** and **precision**.

Accuracy indicates how close a measurement is to the true value.

Precision indicates how close replicate values are to each other.

A good measurement instrument has high accuracy *and* precision if it produces replicate values under constant conditions that vary minimally and are close to the 'true' value.

Example

A blood sample taken from a single individual was divided into four aliquots. A different assay was used on each aliquot to obtain five replicate measures of haemoglobin (g/dl). The 'true' haemoglobin level for this person was known to be 11.0 g/dl. The results obtained with each assay were as follows:

Assay	Replicate measurements	Average	Range	Accuracy	Precision
A	10.9 10.9 11.0 11.1 11.1	11.0	10.9 to 11.1	High	High
B	10.4 10.7 10.8 11.3 11.8	11.0	10.4 to 11.8	High	Low
C	10.3 10.3 10.4 10.5 10.5	10.4	10.3 to 10.5	Low	High
D	10.9 11.2 11.3 11.8 12.3	11.5	10.9 to 12.3	Low	Low

In a sense, accuracy indicates the extent of any systematic influence on the observations and precision indicates the extent of any random influences on the observations.

2.3 Validity

> A measurement method is ***valid*** if it truly measures what it purports to be measuring.

This apparently circular definition is probably best illustrated with an example. A non-invasive test has been developed for measuring blood glucose levels, based on enzyme activity on the skin. If this test is to be considered **valid** for use by people with diabetes to monitor their condition, it must produce the same results as the 'gold standard' (invasive) test which requires a blood test or finger prick test.

In reality, even if the non-invasive test is truly valid, it will produce readings on occasions that differ slightly from the 'gold standard' test readings. This is acceptable provided the differences are not considered to be clinically important. For the new test to be valid the new and 'gold standard' test readings must be done regularly within an acceptable distance of one another (eg on at least 95% of occasions). Validity is frequently impossible to determine directly and has to be assessed indirectly.

3 Probability

3.1 Definitions

THE CONCEPT OF PROBABILITY IS CENTRAL TO STATISTICAL ANALYSIS.

A probability indicates **how likely it is that some event will happen**. Probabilities are computed as fractions, but often reported as percentages. So the following statements, taken from a review of epidemiological studies, are equivalent:

- As many as 40% of adults living in the UK are currently experiencing significant episodes of neck pain.
- The probability that an adult living in the UK is currently experiencing significant episodes of neck pain could be as high as 0.40.
- The probability that an adult living in the UK selected at random from the general population will be currently experiencing significant episodes of neck pain is 0.40.
- In a large random sample of adults living in the UK, we would expect to find that 40% of them are currently experiencing significant episodes of neck pain.

Probabilities are computed in two different ways:

- **A priori** probabilities are determined *theoretically*. A researcher needs to recruit 300 patients with ulcerative colitis for a multi-centre observational safety study of a new drug. A total of 750 eligible patients are currently attending the study centres. If names are drawn truly at random, the probability that any one eligible patient will be invited to take part in the study is 300/750 = 0.40 = 40%.
- **A posteriori** probabilities are determined *empirically* from the frequencies of observed events: 75 of the 300 of the patients recruited into the ulcerative colitis study experienced an adverse event classified as 'non-gastrointestinal'. So, the probability of a

patient with ulcerative colitis experiencing a 'non-gastrointestinal' side-effect when taking the new drug is estimated (for this centre) as being 75/300 = 0.25 = 25%.

Probabilities are often used to summarise qualitative measures in clinical trials. These measures usually are **dichotomous** (ie they have just two categories), but they can also be **polychotomous** (ie have more than two categories).

- Response to treatment – responded/did not respond
- Survival – alive/dead
- Result of a diagnostic test – positive/negative
- Severity of side-effects experienced – nil/mild/moderate/severe

The frequency with which each category arises provides an estimate of the probability of that outcome occurring.

3.2 Properties of probability

A priori and a posteriori probabilities have exactly the same properties (they differ only in the way they are calculated).

- Probabilities take values between 0 and 1 inclusive.
- The probability of an event occurring is 0 (zero) if the event cannot possibly happen.
- The probability of an event occurring is 1 if the event must always happen (ie if no other outcome is possible).
- In real situations, probabilities invariably take a value between 0 and 1.

The 300 patients in the ulcerative colitis study were asked to rate the seriousness of any adverse reactions experienced, using the scale:

nil mild moderate severe

The observed frequencies and (a posteriori) probabilities for the non-gastrointestinal side-effects were:

	Category			
	Nil	Mild	Moderate	Severe
Frequency	225	51	18	6
Probability	225 / 300 = 0.75	54 / 300 = 0.17	18 / 300 = 0.06	6 / 300 = 0.02

> The probabilities of all possible events (categories) **must** always sum to 1.

So, using the simplified notation: p(event) = probability of event occurring,

$$p(\text{no event}) + p(\text{mild event}) + p(\text{moderate event}) + p(\text{severe event})$$

$$= 0.75 + 0.17 + 0.06 + 0.02 = \mathbf{1}$$

3.2.1 Mutually exclusive categories

Categories are defined as being mutually exclusive if they do not overlap in any way (ie outcomes all fall wholly into just one category).

> If categories are mutually exclusive the probability that an event will fall into either of two different categories is the *sum* of the individual probabilities of each category.

$$\boldsymbol{p(\textbf{category 1 or category 2 will occur}) = p(\textbf{category 1 will occur}) + p(\textbf{category 2 will occur})}$$

The categories used in the ulcerative colitis study are clearly mutually exclusive. So, the probability that a patient on the new drug will experience either a mild OR a severe side-effect is:

$$p(\text{mild } \textbf{OR} \text{ severe event}) = p(\text{mild event}) + p(\text{moderate event})$$

$$= 0.17 + 0.06 = 0.23\ (23\%)$$

3.2.2 Independent events

Two events are defined as being independent if the probability of the first event occurring does not influence in any way the probability of the second event occurring.

> If events are independent, the probability that both event 1 AND event 2 will occur is the *product* of the individual probabilities of each event.

$$p(\textbf{category 1 or category 2 will occur}) = p(\textbf{category 1 will occur}) + p(\textbf{category 2 will occur})$$

The side-effects experienced by different patients in the ulcerative colitis study are clearly independent. So, the probability that patient X will experience a mild side-effect AND patient Y will experience a moderate side-effect is:

$$p(\text{patient X has mild side-effect AND patient Y has moderate side-effect})$$

$$= p(\text{patient X has mild side-effect}) + p(\text{patient Y has moderate side-effect})$$

$$= 0.17 \times 0.06 = 0.0102 \text{ (just over 1\%)}$$

3.3 Sensitivity and specificity

Probabilities are also used to good effect to describe the usefulness of a diagnostic test. The extent to which a diagnostic test can distinguish between patients with and without a particular disease is quantified by its sensitivity and specificity.

> **Sensitivity**: proportion of patients with the disease for whom the test will be positive, ie the probability that the test will be positive when the disease is present.
>
> **Specificity**: proportion of patients without the disease for whom

continued overleaf

the test will be negative, ie the probability that the test will be negative when the disease is absent.

Positive predictive value: proportion of positive test results for which the patient does have the disease, ie the probability that, if the test result is positive, the patient truly does have the disease.

Negative predictive value: proportion of negative test results for which the patient does not have the disease, ie the probability that, if the test result is negative, the patient truly does not have the disease.

A diagnostic test is:

- 100% specific if there are no false positive results
- 100% sensitive if there are no false negative results.

There is nearly always a trade-off between sensitivity and specificity – as one increases, the other decreases (or, at best, remains unchanged). Ideally, both sensitivity *and* specificity should achieve desirable levels but frequently only one does so.

Positive and negative predictive values are the most informative clinically, as they provide a direct indication of how accurate the test result obtained actually is. However, sensitivity and specificity are better indicators of the test's usefulness, because:

- Positive and negative predictive values *change* if the prevalence of the disease changes.
- Sensitivity and specificity remain *the same* if the prevalence of the disease changes.

Example

The most commonly reported non-gastrointestinal side-effect reported in the ulcerative colitis study was mild anxiety. This was identified in 56 patients using a simple self-report questionnaire. Because the accuracy of the questionnaire was considered suspect, each of these patients was also interviewed by a psychiatrist. Thus, the 56 patients were each diagnosed as 'anxious' or 'not anxious' on the basis of both a psychiatric interview ('true' diagnosis) and their questionnaire test score ('test' diagnosis). This allows us to examine the accuracy of the questionnaire. (In reality, of course, the accuracy of the test should be

	True (psychiatrist) diagnosis		
	Anxious	Not anxious	Totals
Test (questionnaire) diagnosis			
Anxious	14	3	17
Not anxious	5	34	39
Totals	19	37	56

determined by a much larger sample than is used in this illustrative example).

$$\text{Sensitivity} = 14/19 = 0.737\ (73.7\%)$$

$$\text{Specificity} = 34/37 = 0.919\ (91.9\%)$$

$$\text{Positive predictive value} = 14/17 = 0.824\ (82.4\%)$$

$$\text{Negative predictive value} = 34/39 = 0.872\ (87.2\%)$$

The test is slightly better at correctly diagnosing patients who are not anxious than those who are.

Which is more important – sensitivity or specificity?

This is usually determined by the clinical context in which the test will be used. For example:

- When using a screening test for neonatal hypothyroidism or phenylketonuria, a number of false positive results might be acceptable, but false negatives (missed diagnoses) would lead to the failure to treat the conditions early with irreversible consequences – in this situation, sensitivity is more important than specificity.
- When undertaking tilt-table testing for episodes of syncope, a false negative result might be acceptable if the symptoms are currently minor and/or infrequent, but a false positive (incorrect diagnosis) could result in a patient receiving a permanent pacemaker unnecessarily – in this situation, specificity is more important than sensitivity.

4 Important distributions

4.1 What is a distribution?

As discussed at length in Chapter 1, observations vary, often considerably. The exact nature of this variation – that is, the way in which the observations *distribute* themselves over the range of possible values – depends on the type of measure being used.

Observations can have one of very many different types of statistical distribution. Fortunately, a small number of these tend to occur frequently.

BEFORE EMBARKING ON THE VOYAGE OF DISCOVERY THAT IS 'STATISTICAL ANALYSIS', CAREFUL CONSIDERATION OF THE DISTRIBUTION OF EACH OF THE MEASURES COLLECTED IN A STUDY IS ESSENTIAL.

4.2 Binomial distribution

In many clinical trials, the outcome for each patient is reduced to just two possible outcomes, for example:

- Response to treatment – responded/did not respond
- Survival – alive/dead
- Result of a diagnostic test – positive/negative.

Qualitative measures that have only two categories are called **binary variables**.

Example

A definitive meta-analysis has been carried out combining the results of all known clinical studies involving a new drug for the treatment of gastric ulcer. In every study, patients were classified at the end of four weeks of treatment as having an ulcer that was 'healed' or 'not healed'.

Binary variables such as this are usually summarised by reporting the proportions (or probabilities) of patients in each category.

So, if the total proportion of patients in the meta-analysis found to have a healed ulcer was 'p_1', the proportion p_1 can be interpreted as: the (estimated) probability that a new patient with a gastric ulcer will respond to this drug if treated for four weeks.

Suppose $p_1 = 0.70$. That is, 70% of patients responded to the treatment. If we treat a new sample of 10 patients with the drug, as each patient constitutes an independent event and each has the same theoretical probability (0.70) of being healed:

- On average, we would expect $(10 \times 0.70) = 7$ of the patients to be 'healed'.
- In reality, because of random variation, the actual number 'healed' may be different from 7.
- If several samples of 10 patients are treated with the drug, the number 'healed' will vary from sample to sample.

The exact nature of this variation can be determined theoretically by using the properties of probabilities described in the Chapter 3. The probabilities of different numbers of patients being 'healed' in a random sample of 10 patients are:

Number healed	0	1	2	3	4	5
Probability	<0.001	<0.001	0.001	0.009	0.037	0.103
Number healed	6	7	8	9	10	
Probability	0.200	0.267	0.233	0.121	0.028	

These probabilities form a **probability distribution**. The most likely outcome is that 7 patients will be 'healed', but on average this will occur for just over a quarter (26.7%) of samples. It is almost as likely that 6 or 8 patients will be 'healed'.

> The probability distribution for a binary variable is called a **binomial distribution**.

The shape of a binomial distribution is determined by the value of the parameter 'p' (ie by the probability of success for an individual patient). Figure 1 shows three different binomial distributions for a larger group of 20 patients.

- The first graph assumes a 'healed' rate of $p = 0.25$.
- The second graph assumes a 'healed' rate of $p = 0.50$.
- The third graph assumes a 'healed' rate of $p = 0.75$.

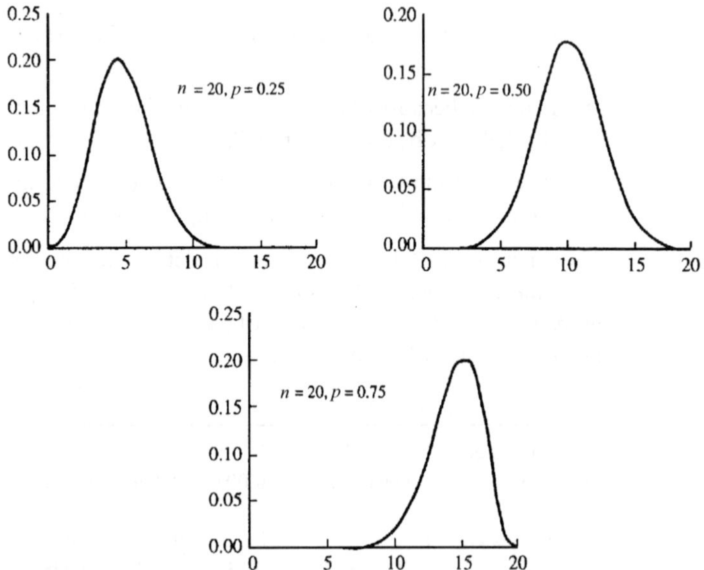

Figure 1 Three examples of the binomial distribution

4.3 Poisson distribution

Many discrete continuous measures arise from counting the number of events which occur:

- in a **fixed time interval** (eg the number of epileptic fits experienced by a patient in one year)
- in a **fixed space** (eg the numbers of cells in a graticule on a microscope field/slide).

Such measures have a theoretical Poisson distribution.

The exact shape of a Poisson distribution is characterised by the mean number of events that occur in a unit period of time/a unit space.

The variance of a Poisson distribution is equal to the mean.

4.4 Normal (Gaussian) distribution

NB: This section assumes knowledge of the following statistics: mean, median, mode, standard deviation, variance. If you are unfamiliar with these, you may find it helpful to read Chapter 5 now.

MANY CONTINUOUS BIOLOGICAL MEASURES HAVE AN (APPROXIMATE) NORMAL DISTRIBUTION.

The mathematical formula for the Normal distribution was derived by the French mathematician Gauss, so this is sometimes referred to as a **Gaussian** distribution.

An example of a Normal distribution is shown in Figure 2.

A Normal distribution is:

- characterised by being 'bell-shaped' (unimodal) and symmetrical about its central value
- completely defined by its mean and variance.

Possibly the most frequently asked question during a statistical analysis is: How can I tell if my (continuous) observations have a Normal distribution? In a sense, this question is meaningless. The Normal distribution is just a theoretical mathematical formula. Observations can only approximate to this distribution.

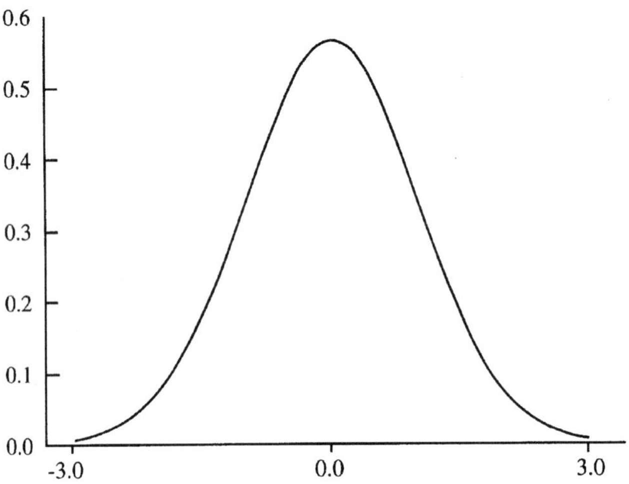

Figure 2 The (standard) Normal/Gaussian distribution

The question would be better stated as: Do my observations approximate sufficiently closely to a Normal distribution for me to assume that they have such a distribution?

There are some sophisticated statistical procedures for answering this question. For most practical purposes, however, an adequate answer can be obtained by considering some important properties of a Normal distribution.

- A histogram of the observations (see Chapter 6) should look very similar to Figure 2.
- Because the normal distribution is symmetrical:

  mean = median = mode

- Fixed proportions of observations lie within stated ranges on either side of the mean (Figure 3). The most important of these are:
  - 68.2% (fractionally over two-thirds) of observations lie within 1 standard deviation
  - 95% of observations lie within 1.96 standard deviations
  - 95.5% (ie fractionally over 95%) of observations lie within 2 standard deviations (ie less than 5% of observations are further

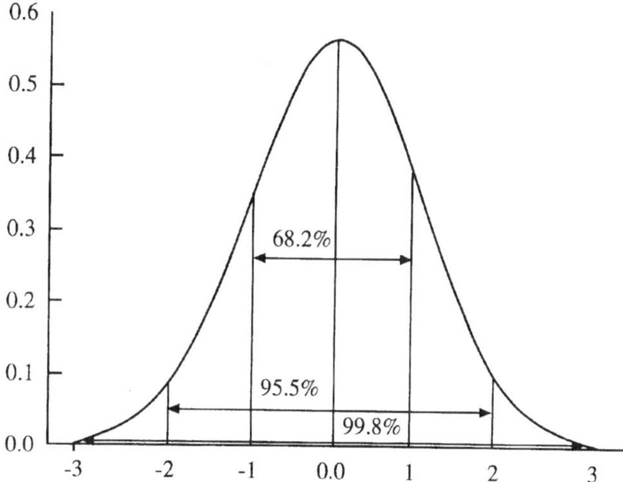

Figure 3 The (standard) Normal/Gaussian distribution: proportions of observations between 1, 2 and 3 standard deviations of mean value

than 2 standard deviations away from the mean)

- 99.8% (virtually all) of the observations lie within 3 standard deviations.

If a set of observations can be reasonably said to have all of the above properties, they can be considered to adequately approximate to a Normal distribution. However, if they seriously violate any one of these properties, they cannot be assumed to have a Normal distribution.

For large sample sizes the binomial distribution approximates to a normal distribution with:

$$\boldsymbol{mean = np} \text{ and } \boldsymbol{variance = np(1-p)}$$

(where n is the sample size and p is the binomial probability).

The Poisson distribution approximates to a Normal distribution with mean = variance.

4.5 Standard Normal distribution

A Normal distribution is defined by its mean and variance – both of which can take an infinite number of different values. As there are thus an infinite number of different Normal distributions, constructing tables showing the properties of all possible Normal distributions would be a very time consuming task. Fortunately:

- Observations from all Normal distributions can be converted into a **standard Normal distribution**.
- This is done by subtracting the mean of the distribution from each observation and then dividing these differences by the standard deviation of the distribution.

A set of observations (X) have a Normal distribution with mean μ and variance σ^2. A new set of observations are calculated from these as follows:

$$Z = (X - \mu)/\sigma = (X - \text{mean})/\text{standard deviation}$$

These observations (Z) have a standard Normal distribution, which has mean 0 and variance 1.

Thus, tables which detail the properties of the standard Normal distribution can be used for observations with any Normal distribution.

A cautionary word

Biological measures usually (*normally*) produce observations that approximate very closely to the Gaussian distribution. It is perhaps not too surprising, therefore, that the distribution became widely known as the Normal distribution. This should not be confused with the concept of clinical normality. Thus:

- Haemoglobin levels may follow a statistically Normal distribution, but a value of 8 mg/dl is *clinically abnormal* and indicates the likely presence of a disease state.
- Resting pulse rates may follow a statistically non-Normal distribution, but a value of 72 beats/min is clinically normal.

4.6 Student *t*-distribution

> A measure produces observations that have a theoretical Normal distribution with mean μ and variance σ^2.
>
> If n randomly selected individuals are measured the mean of their observations will also have a theoretical Normal distribution, with the same mean μ but with a much *smaller* variance σ^2/n.

In practice, this holds for large samples, but when the sample size is small:

- the value of the (population) variance tends to be under-estimated
- the sample means have a distribution that is symmetrical, but has slightly longer tails (ie has greater spread) than would be expected for a Normal distribution.

Opinions differ over what constitutes a **small** sample. In general, however, these problems are often discernible for samples involving 60 observations or less (ie if $n \leq 60$).

The exact mathematical form of the distribution of the means for small samples drawn from a Normal distribution was derived in 1908 by WS Gossett. Because of a dispute with his employers (the Guinness brewery in Dublin), Gossett was forced to publish under the pseudonym 'Student'. Consequently, this distribution is known universally as the **Student *t*-distribution**.

The amount of spread (variation) in a Student *t*-distribution depends on the number of *degrees of freedom* for the variance estimate. As the sample size increases, the Student *t*-distribution increasingly resembles the standard Normal distribution, until eventually the two distributions are virtually indistinguishable from each other.

4.7 Non-Normal (continuous) distributions

Some biological variables follow distributions that are **unimodal** (ie have a single mode value) but are not symmetrical. Observations with this property have a **skewed distribution**.

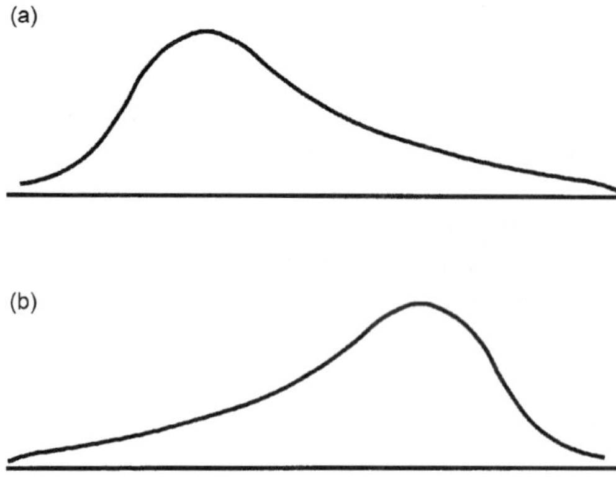

Figure 4 (a) Positively skewed, continuous distribution. (b) Negatively skewed, continuous distribution

A distribution which has:

- a long tail on the right (ie a tendency for observations to range further above the mode than below the mode) is **positively skewed** (Figure 4a)
- a long tail on the left (ie a tendency for observations to range further below the mode than above the mode) is **negatively skewed** (Figure 4b).

It is important to know the relative size of the mean, median and mode for Normal and non-Normal distributions:

- For observations that are Normally distributed: mean = median = mode
- for observations that are non-Normal and *positively* skewed: mean ≥ median > mode
- for observations that are non-Normal and *negatively* skewed: mean ≤ median < mode

These relationships are not as difficult to remember as they may seem.

- Observations that are Normally distributed: the three averages are equal.
- Observations that are skewed: the three averages are different (Figure 5).

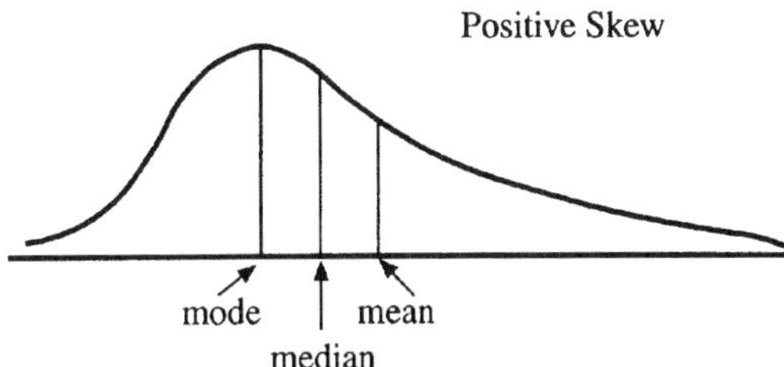

Figure 5 Skewed continuous distribution: relationship between mode, median and mean

However, positively and negatively skewed distributions are effectively mirror images about the mode, so the relationships are identical but reversed.

- The mode is the most commonly occurring value (see Chapter 5) so is always at the apex of the distribution.
- The mean is most affected by extreme observations, so is pulled away from the mode in the direction of the skewness.
- The median is less affected by extreme observations, so is between the mode and the mean.

4.8 Log-Normal (continuous) distributions

Many biological measures produce observations with a particular type of positively skewed distribution known as the **log-Normal distribution**. The most important – and most useful – property of this distribution is that it can be **transformed** (converted) into a Normal distribution by simply taking the (natural) logarithm of each observation. In this situation, the statistical analysis is carried out using the logarithms of the original observations. Most (but not all) of the summary statistics produced with these can be **detransformed** back into the original units by computing their anti-logs (exponentials).

4.9 Normalising transformations

In most situations, continuous observations with a distribution that is skewed and unimodal can be transformed into a Normal distribution. That is, some mathematical function can be applied to the original observations to produce a new set of observations that have an (approximate) Normal distribution. These functions are known as **normalising transformations**.

Complex statistical tests have been developed to determine the most appropriate Normalising transformation for any particular set of observations. Statistical analysis methods appropriate for Normally distributed data are used on the transformed (normalised) values. Under certain circumstances, the results of these analyses can then be detransformed back into the original units for presentation.

Normalising transformations are a very powerful weapon in the statistical armory, but are complex to use and should be handled with great care and caution. Expert statistical assistance should be sought if such a transformation is considered desirable.

Examples of the more common transformations used with biological measures are given below:

- Observations with a Poisson or similar distribution (such as counts or the number of times an event occurs in a fixed time period) are often only moderately positively skewed – these can sometimes be Normalised by taking the square root of each observation.
- Observations that are more positively skewed often have a log-Normal distribution and can be Normalised by taking the natural logarithms of each observation (see Section 4.8).

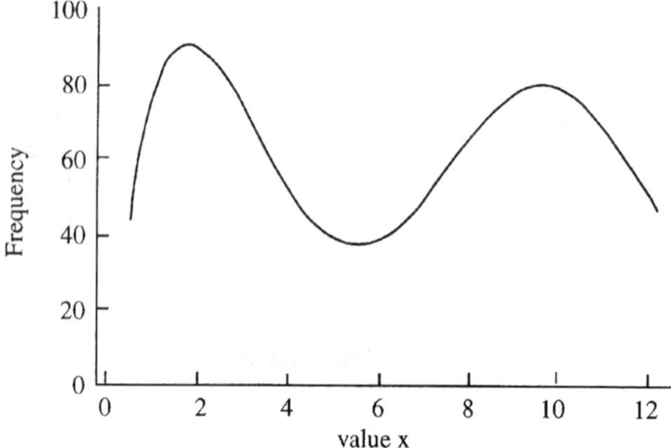

Figure 6 Bimodal frequency distribution

- Observations that are negatively skewed can sometimes be Normalised using the reciprocal transformation (1/observation).
- Observations that are proportions (percentages) are often positively skewed if their average is close to 0 or negatively skewed if their average is close to 1 (100%). In both situations, the skewness is caused by the range of possible values being constrained at 0 and 1 (100%). Such observations can sometimes be converted into a Normal distribution by using one of several complex mathematical transformations (eg arcsine, probit, logit).

If a set of observations has two modal values, the distribution is said to be bimodal (eg Figure 6). No transformation will Normalise this type of distribution.

5 Basic descriptive statistics

5.1 Importance of descriptive statistics

THE IMPORTANCE OF GOOD DESCRIPTIVE STATISTICS CANNOT BE OVER-EMPHASISED.

The basic results of any study, whether observational or a clinical trial, are identified by computing appropriate descriptive/summary statistics. Once these are known, tentative conclusions can be drawn. All subsequent analyses are essentially carried out to establish the confidence with which these conclusions can be made.

The author once spent considerable time on the telephone trying to explain the interpretation of a *p*-value to a researcher who had completed a comparative trial of two drugs. Eventually, it became apparent that he did in fact understand this concept totally. His confusion was due to the fact that he had a 'significant' *p*-value, but he could not interpret it because he had not computed any summary statistics. Without estimates of the effects of the two drugs, the sophisticated (and perfectly correct) analysis carried out to obtain the *p*-value was rendered meaningless.

The descriptive statistics appropriate in any given situation depend on the type of measure.

5.2 Descriptive statistics for qualitative/categorical data

> The only descriptive statistics appropriate for qualitative measures are **frequency counts.**

The numbers of observations falling into each category (frequency counts) usually provide a totally comprehensive summary of a qualitative variable. Thus, the following table fully summarises the results of an observational survey of 800 patients with arthritis to determine the prevalence of three diagnostic groupings.

	Diagnosis		
	Osteoarthritis	Rheumatoid arthritis	Psoriatic arthritis
Number of patients	376	312	112

Unfortunately, frequency counts on their own do not always readily describe the study findings as clearly as might be desired. To achieve this, showing the frequencies as proportions, or more informatively as percentages, can be extremely effective.

	Diagnosis		
	Osteoarthritis	Rheumatoid arthritis	Psoriatic arthritis
Number of patients	376 (47%)	312 (39%)	112 (14%)

The advantage of percentages is even more dramatically seen in the context of clinical trials. The following table shows the numbers of patients responding to two treatments in a (small) comparative clinical trial.

Treatment group	Responders	Non-responders	Total sample
A	22	25	47
B	23	29	52

Visibly, the response rates are similar for both treatments, so the difference between them is unlikely to be statistically significant. But it is not immediately obvious just how large (or small) the difference actually is. Adding percentages provides this information clearly and succinctly.

Treatment group	Responders	Non-responders	Total sample
A	22 (47%)	25 (53%)	47
B	23 (44%)	29 (56%)	52

The actual frequency counts should *always* be reported with percentages/proportions. Percentages/proportions on their own can be inadvertently misleading.

Suppose the response rate to a standard treatment is widely established as being approximately 25%. A paper presented at a conference has suggested that, in an ongoing clinical trial, early indication of the response rate for a new treatment is 80%. The new treatment appears to be a major therapeutic breakthrough. However, the (statistical *and* clinical) strength of this claim differs hugely depending on whether:

- 4 (80%) patients have so far responded out of 5 treated, or
- 800 (80%) patients have so far responded out of 1000 treated.

Statistical analyses must *always* be performed using the actual frequency counts. Using the percentages/proportions will produce incorrect and/or misleading conclusions.

5.2.1 Odds ratios/relative incidence ratios

Odds ratios and incidence ratios are used widely to summarise categorical measures. These two statistics are particularly useful for evaluating factors that might be influencing categorical measures (see Chapter 10, Section 10.4).

Odds ratios

In the comparative study summarised above:

- Odds of responding for treatment group A
= (probability of responding)/(probability of not responding)
= (number of responders)/(number of non-responders)
= 22/25 = 0.88 (88%)
- Odds of responding for treatment group B = 23/29 = 0.79 (79%)
- The odds ratio (for group A relative to group B) = 0.88/0.79 = 1.11
- The odds ratio (for group B relative to group A) = 0.79/0.88 = 0.90

The odds of responding is 1.11 times greater (11% greater) for treatment A compared with (relative to) treatment B.

Incidence ratios

In the comparative study summarised above:

- Incidence of responders for treatment group A
= probability of responding
= (number of responders)/(total sample)
= 22/47 = 0.47 (47%)
- Incidence of responders for treatment group B = 23/52 = 0.44 (44%)
- Incidence ratio (for group A relative to group B) = 0.47/0.44 = 1.06
- Incidence ratio (for group B relative to group A) = 0.44/0.47 = 0.94

The incidence of responders is 1.06 times greater (6% greater) for treatment A compared with (relative to) treatment B.

5.3 Descriptive statistics for quantitative data

Quantitative measures, such as blood pressure and blood test levels, have to be summarised using two descriptive statistics:

- a measure of central tendency (**average**)
- a measure of dispersion (**variation**).

These will be illustrated using the following (fictitious) data set: 15 migraine sufferers were recruited into a clinical trial. During a 3-month run-in period to establish the baseline severity of the condition, the numbers of attacks reported were as follows.

3	1	1	2	12	1	7	2	4	1	2	4	1	3	1

5.3.1 Measures of central tendency

Several measures of central tendency are commonly used in medical statistics.

> **Arithmetic mean**: the sum of the observations divided by the number of observations.

Arithmetic mean =

$$(3 + 1 + 1 + 2 + 12 + 1 + 7 + 2 + 4 + 1 + 2 + 4 + 1 + 3 + 1)/15 = 45/15 = \mathbf{3}$$

The mean should only be used when the observations can be assumed to have a Normal distribution (see Chapter 4), ie, the observations range symmetrically around the mean. In this example, the observations are clearly not symmetrical about the mean, so the arithmetic mean is not an appropriate summary statistic.

> **Geometric mean**: The nth root of the product of the observations (where n is the number of observations).

Geometric mean =

$$(3.\ 1.\ 1.\ 2.\ 12.\ 1.\ 7.\ 2.\ 4.\ 1.\ 2.\ 4.\ 1.\ 3.\ 1)^{15} = 96768^{15} = \mathbf{2.15}$$

The geometric mean should only be used when the observations are positively skewed and can be assumed to have a log-Normal distribution (see Chapter 4). In this example, the observations are indeed positively skewed (and do have a reasonable log-Normal distribution), so the geometric mean is an appropriate summary statistic.

Some mathematical problems are associated with the geometric mean:

- If just one observation is zero, the geometric mean must also be zero.
- The geometric mean cannot be calculated at all if any of the observations are negative. In this situation, a sufficiently large constant value has to be added to all of the observations to make them positive.

Expert statistical advice should be sought if the geometric mean is to be used.

> **Median**: the value which divides the observations into two equal halves when they are arranged in order of increasing value.

Median	1	1	1	1	1	1	2	**2**	2	3	3	4	4	7	12

The median can be used irrespective of the way the observations distribute themselves. The median is an appropriate summary statistic for these observations.

> **Mode**: the most commonly occurring value.

In this example mode = **1**.

The mode is rarely used in practice, because:

- it can be difficult to estimate for very large sets of observations, as many different values may occur with equal frequency
- some data distributions naturally have several modal values
- for observations that are counts or ordinal categories, the mode is often at one end of the data range.

The mode is **not** an appropriate summary statistic for these observations.

5.3.2 Measures of dispersion (variation): Normally distributed observations

For quantitative measures, knowing the average is only part of the picture. Knowledge of the extent to which the observations vary from one another is also important.

If a continuous measure produces observations that vary symmetrically about their mean value (ie can be reasonably approximated to a Normal distribution – see Chapter 4), the most informative measure of dispersion is the average distance each individual observation differs (**deviates**) from the mean value.

In practice, this is much more difficult to calculate than you might imagine. But then, no-one ever said that statistics were easy!

The problems are best illustrated with the following diagram, which represents a series of observations from some continuous measure.

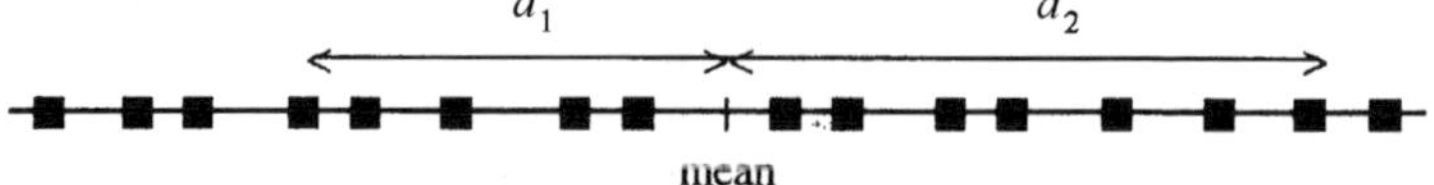

The deviations of these observations are computed as follows:

Deviation of observation 1
$= d_1 =$ (value of observation 1 – mean value)

Deviation of observation 2
$= d_2 =$ (value of observation 2 – mean value)

and so on .... The **average deviation** is the arithmetic mean of these *d* values (differences). However:

- The observations below the mean will all have *negative* deviations.
- The observations above the mean will all have *positive* deviations.

Because of the mathematics involved, when the average of the deviations is calculated, the positive and negative deviations will always cancel each other out exactly.

So the average deviation will always be zero. This statistic is easy to calculate, but is not exactly informative.

Variance

To resolve this problem, the negative values have to be made positive. Intuitively, just simply ignoring the minus signs might seem the obvious thing to do, but this just creates a different set of mathematical problems.

The problem is actually resolved by squaring the deviations. The squares of all numbers, whether positive or negative, are positive. For example:

$$3^2 = 9 \text{ and } -3^2 = 9$$

When these squared deviations are added together (summed), they must give a value that is greater than zero. (The sum can actually equal zero, but only when all the deviations are zero, ie when the observations are all equal.)

This statistic is the **sum of squares about the mean** (usually shortened to **sum of squares**). It indicates the size, but not the direction, of the deviations.

> **Variance**: average (mean) of the squared deviations

If an entire target clinical population has been studied, the population mean is known exactly. In this situation, the variance is calculated by dividing the sum of the squared deviations by the total sample size (n).

Usually, however, only a sample of people from the target population is studied, so the population mean has to be estimated from the sample observations. At this point, the calculations are in danger of imploding in on themselves!

Certainly, this creates a mathematical problem, the consequence of which is that if the squared deviations are divided by the sample size (n), the value obtained is *biased* and tends to under-estimate the true variance value. Fortunately, this problem is easily resolved, by the simple process of dividing the sum of the squared deviations by the number of observations minus 1 (ie by $n - 1$).

> **Variance**: sum of squares about the mean/(number of observations – 1)

- The units of the variance are the units of the measure squared.
- The variance is defined as having $(n - 1)$ *degrees of freedom*.

Standard deviation

The variance estimates the average *squared* distance each individual observation deviates from the mean value. The estimate needed is just the *average* distance each individual observation deviates from the mean value. The intuitively obvious way of doing this is to simply take the square root of the variance. Doing so produces the statistic known as the *standard deviation*.

> **Standard deviation**: square root of the variance (√ variance).

In strict mathematical terms, taking the square root of the variance in this way does *not* produce the desired statistic. For most practical purposes, however, the value obtained is acceptably close to this statistic.

> So, as a working definition: standard deviation can be regarded as being equal to the average distance each individual observation lies away (deviates) from the sample mean

The standard deviation has the same units as the observations.

Standard error

The standard error is defined as the standard deviation divided by the square root of the sample size (n). This statistic provides invaluable information about the accuracy of sample estimates and is described in proper detail when confidence intervals are considered (Chapter 7).

Standard error = standard deviation/$\sqrt{n}$

Coefficient of variation

Standard deviation is a measure of precision. If several different methods are available for measuring the same entity (eg laboratory assays), it might be appropriate to select the one with the best precision. But if the methods all have different units, the standard deviations are not directly comparable.

In this situation, a better measure of precision is provided by the coefficient of variation. This is the ratio of the standard deviation and mean, and is usually expressed as a percentage. It is unit free.

Coefficient of variation = (standard deviation/mean) × 100

5.3.3 Measures of dispersion (variation): non-Normally distributed observations

If the observations are not distributed symmetrically around the mean value, the statistics described in the previous section are unsuitable. The most appropriate measure of dispersion in this situation is the **range**. This is simply the smallest and largest observation in the sample.

Range: the smallest and largest observations in the sample.

5.3.4 Quantiles

Sometimes, presenting a single measure of spread such as the standard deviation is not enough. For example, to clinically interpret a patient's lung function test, it is important to know where their test result lies within the range of values that can be expected from a normal healthy individual. In this situation, more detail is needed about how lung function test results distribute themselves over the whole range of possible values. This is achieved succinctly by computing **quantiles**.

> **Quantiles**: values that divide a distribution into segments in such a way that there are specific proportions of observations *below* each quantile.

Three types of quantile are used widely.

- The **median** is the quantile that divides a distribution into two equal parts. The median is the central value of the distribution (see above), so 50% of observations lie below the median. By definition, 50% of observations also lie above the median.
- **Quartiles** divide a distribution into four equal parts:
  - 25% of observations lie below the first (lower) quartile (Q25)
  - 50% of observations lie below the second (middle) quartile (the median)
  - 75% of observations lie below the third (upper) quartile (Q75).

Thus, the four segments defined by the quartiles each contain 25% of the distribution. The distance between the lower and upper quartiles (the central 50% of the distribution) is often referred to as the **interquartile range**.

- **Percentiles (centiles)** divide a distribution into 100 equal parts:
  - 10% of observations lie below the 10th percentile
  - 50% of observations lie below the 50th percentile (median)
  - 95% of observations lie below the 95th percentile, and so on.

Thus, 1% of observations lie between consecutive percentiles.

Percentiles are used widely to define the normal ranges for clinical measures. Usually, if observations have:

- a Normal distribution – quantiles are computed theoretically from the properties of this distribution.
- a non-Normal distribution – quantiles are computed empirically from the actual observations.

5.3.5 Effect size

When comparing the results of two studies testing the same two interventions (A and B), it may be difficult if the studies have used different outcome measures (or different units for the same measure). In this situation, it is useful to compute the effect size (**standardised mean difference**).

Effect size = (mean for intervention A – mean for intervention b)/standard deviation

6 Graphical presentation of data

STATISTICS ARE USUALLY INHERENTLY BORING.

A picture is worth ten thousand words

Frederick R Barnard

6.1 Qualitative measures

Example

Of 1000 patients with arthritis entered into a clinical trial, 500 had osteoarthritis, 350 had rheumatoid arthritis and 150 had psoriatic arthritis. These results are shown as a **pie diagram** (Figure 7a) and a **bar chart** (Figure 7b).

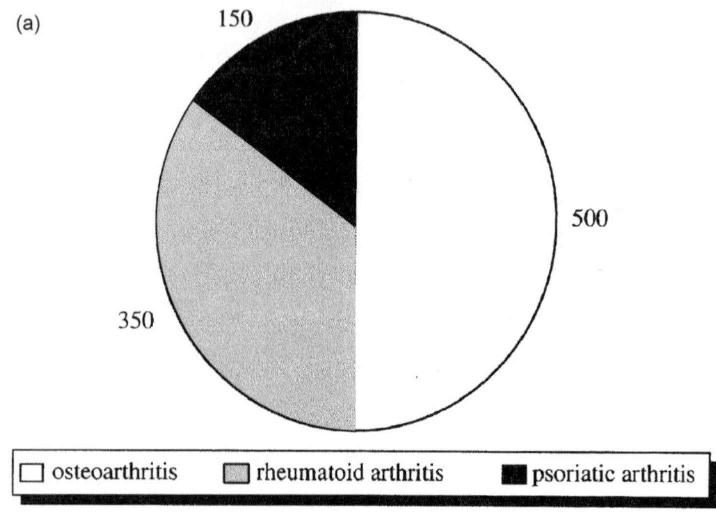

Figure 7 (a) Pie chart of arthritis diagnosis group frequencies

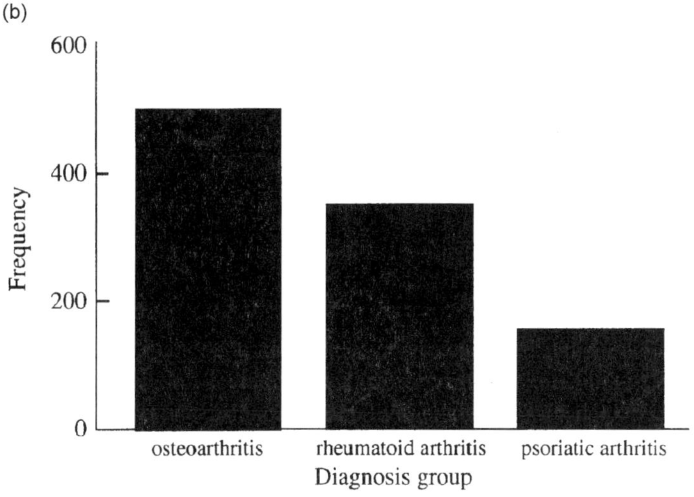

Figure 7 (b) Bar chart of arthritis diagnosis group frequencies

6.2 Quantitative data

A variety of graphical methods exist for displaying quantitative data.

> **Dot diagrams**: show the distribution of the observations obtained from different subject groups by displaying each individual data point.

Example

A new biochemical test has been devised for helping in the diagnosis of a disease. Test results have been obtained for 44 patients known not to have the disease and 36 patients in whom the diagnosis was certain. The results of this study are shown in the form of a dot diagram in Figure 8.

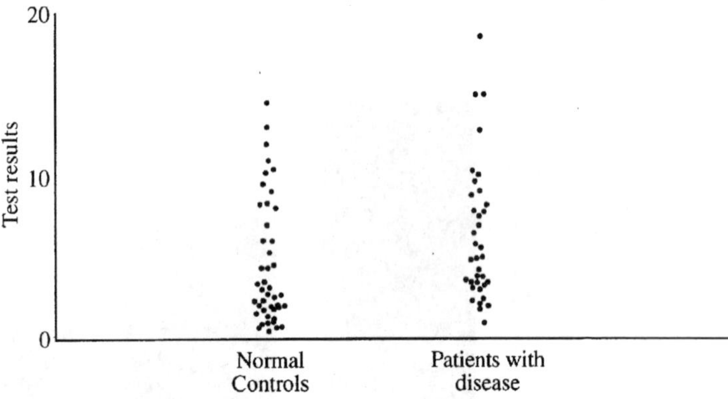

Figure 8 Dot diagram

Placing the dot diagrams adjacently on the same scale shows that:

- the test result tends to be fractionally higher for patients with the disease
- the amount of overlap between the groups is too great for the method to provide a clinically useful diagnostic test.

> **Histograms**: show a series of bars, each bar corresponding to a particular range of test results.

The area of each bar represents the number (or percentage) of patients within that range. All of the bars should have the same width, so that the length of the bar represents the number (or percentage) of patients with a result within a particular range. (There are situations in which it is acceptable to break this rule, but these are rare.)

Example

Measurements of inflamed joints were taken from 150 patients with psoriatic arthritis (Figure 9).

- The height of each histogram bar represents the number of patients with a particular number of affected joints.
- Four patients had just one swollen joint, eight had two swollen joints, and so on.

Histograms appear deceptively simple, but the rules concerning their construction are actually quite complex.

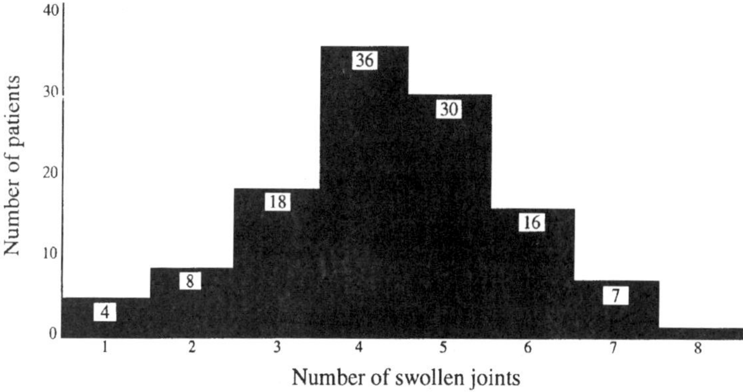

Figure 9 Histogram - number of psoriatic arthritis with one or more swollen joints

Frequency distributions: also show the frequency with which (groups of) observations occurs.

In this type of graph only the tops of the histogram bars are shown. These are joined to produce a (smooth) curve.

If drawn using percentages rather than frequencies on the vertical axis, the graph produced is called a **relative frequency distribution**.

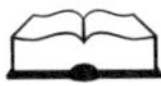

Example

The numbers of inflamed joints in the group of 150 patients with psoriatic arthritis are shown as a frequency distribution in Figure 10.

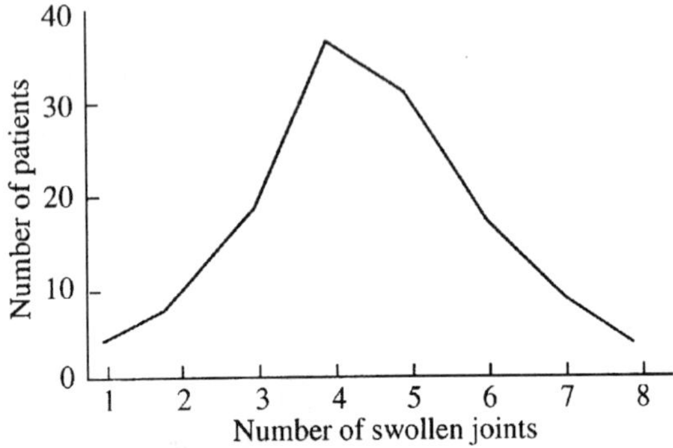

Figure 10 Frequency distribution – number of psoriatic arthritic patients with one or more swollen joints

---

Box-and-whisker plots: used extensively in clinical journals to graphically describe the distribution of measures (Figure 11). They are particularly effective for comparing sub-groups.

- The **box** element of the plot shows the quartiles, with the median marked as a line within the box (ie the top and bottom of the box represents the 75th and 25th percentiles respectively, while the line within the box represents the 50th percentile).
- The **whisker** element of the plot shows the maximum and minimum observation values.

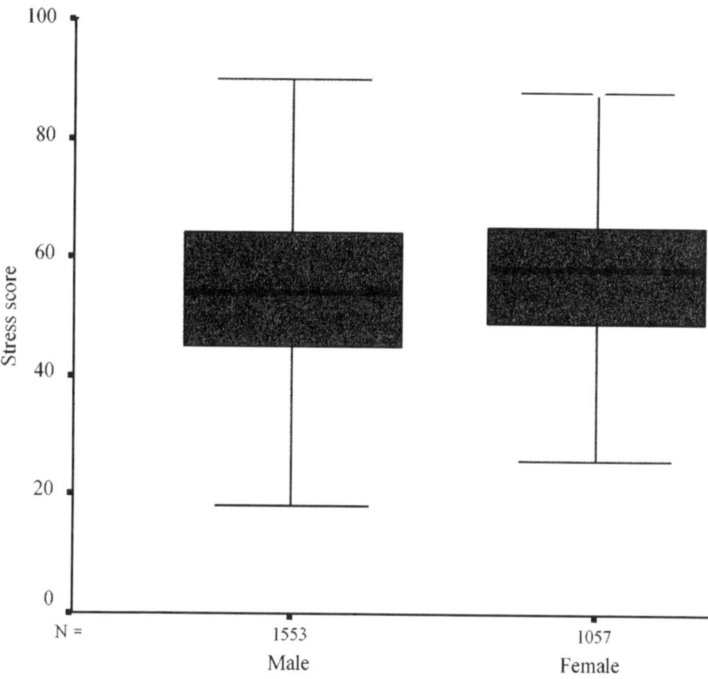

Figure 11 Box-and-whisker plots of stress scores for civil servants

7 Confidence intervals

7.1 General concept

ALL RESULTS OBTAINED FROM A CLINICAL STUDY SHOULD BE PRESENTED WITH THEIR CONFIDENCE INTERVALS.

Clinical studies can rarely include all patients in the target population. Instead, a sample of patients has to be studied. This sample is used as a proxy for the whole population.

A sample of 250 individuals was selected at random from the general population of hypertensive patients. Each was prescribed a new drug to lower their diastolic blood pressure (DBP).

- The mean change in DBP will provide an *estimate* of the true (average) effect of the drug
- The proportion of patients who experience an unwanted side-effect will provide an *estimate* of the true toxicity risk for the drug.

The importance of the fact that the results obtained are **estimates** cannot be over-emphasised. Because of sampling error (and the other sources of error discussed in detail in Chapter 1), the estimates are likely to be incorrect (although hopefully not by much).

- The mean change in DBP will be similar to, but not exactly equal to, the true (average) effect of the drug.
- The proportion of patients who experience an unwanted side-effect will be similar to, but not exactly equal to, the true toxicity risk for the drug.

> A properly selected random sample will be representative of the study population – the characteristics of the sample will be similar to (but not identical to) those of the whole population and will produce estimates very close to, but not necessarily equal to, the true population value.

If the study is well conducted, the error in the estimates should be small. Nevertheless, the likely effect of this error should be considered. By taking proper consideration of the variation in the study observations, the likely amount of error in the study estimates can be quantified.

The error in an estimate is best represented by an appropriate **confidence interval**, because this:

- provides a measure of the extent to which a sample estimate is likely to differ from the true population value (ie it is a measure of the degree of precision/uncertainty associated with the sample estimate)
- indicates, with a stated level of certainty (usually 95%), the range of values within which the true population mean is likely to lie.

7.2 Standard errors

Before looking at how confidence intervals are calculated, more knowledge is needed about the concept of **standard error**, which was introduced in Chapter 5, Section 5.3.2.

7.2.1 Quantitative data

Standard errors should be computed only for continuous measures only if that can be assumed to have a Normal distribution.

Suppose several random samples, each consisting of 250 hypertensive patients, were selected in the same way from the same population. All patients in each sample were prescribed the new DBP-lowering drug. If the changes in DBP can be assumed to follow a Normal distribution:

- the mean change experienced by the patients in any one of these samples will provide an estimate of the therapeutic efficacy of the drug

- the estimates of therapeutic efficacy obtained from these samples will be similar but not necessarily equal.

The amount and shape of variation in these means is called the **sampling distribution** of the sample means.

As already stated in Chapter 4, Section 4.6, if single observations have a theoretical Normal distribution with mean μ and variance σ^2, the means of random samples of n observations will also follow a Normal distribution with the same mean μ but much smaller variance σ^2/n.

The **standard error** of the sample mean **(SEM)** is defined as:
$SEM = \sigma/\sqrt{n}$.

- The SEM is equal to the standard deviation of the individual observations divided by the square root of the number of observations in the sample.
- The standard error is smaller than the standard deviation (except when the sample is just a single observation, ie when $n = 1$)
- The standard error indicates the extent to which sample means vary (spread) around the true population mean.
- The standard deviation indicates the extent to which individual observations vary (spread) around the true population mean.
- Mathematically, the standard deviation is the special case of the standard error when $n = 1$ (ie standard deviation is the standard error for samples consisting of a single observation).

As sample size (n) increases:

- the standard error decreases in size
- the sample mean becomes an increasingly better (closer) estimate of the true population mean
- the sample standard deviation becomes an increasingly better (closer) estimate of the true population standard deviation.

The population variance is usually unknown, so has to be estimated from the study sample. For a random sample of size n:

- the sample variance (usually denoted by s^2) is computed as described in Chapter 5, Section 5.3.2.
- the sample standard deviation is s
- the sample SEM is $s/\sqrt{n}$.

7.2.2 Qualitative data

As in the previous section, several random samples, each consisting of 250 hypertensive patients, were selected in the same way from the same population. All patients in each sample were prescribed the new DBP-lowering drug.

- The proportion of patients in any one of these samples who experienced an unwanted side-effect will provide an estimate of the toxicity risk level for the drug.
- Again, the estimates of toxicity risk level obtained from each of the samples will be similar but not necessarily equal.

In a sample of n individuals, if the number falling into a particular category (in this instance, who experience a side-effect) is r, the proportion (p) falling into this category is calculated as:

$$p = r/n$$

For small samples

The sampling distribution of p is determined exactly using the properties of the binomial distribution.

For large samples

The distribution of the observed proportions (p) around the true population proportion approximates closely to a Normal distribution with:

- mean p
- variance $p(1-p)/n$
- standard error $\sqrt{[p(1-p)/n]}$

7.3 Computing confidence intervals

7.3.1 Confidence intervals for a Normal distribution (quantitative data)

As described previously in Chapter 4, Section 4.4, fixed proportions of observations with a Normal distribution lie within stated ranges either side of the population mean (see Figure 3). For example:

- 68.2% of observations lie within 1 standard deviation
- 95% of observations lie within 1.96 standard deviations
- 99.8% of observations lie within 3 standard deviations

In general, α% of observations lie within z^{α} standard deviations either side of the mean (where z^{α} is the appropriate percentile value from the standard Normal distribution). If α% of observations lie within z^{α} standard deviations either side of the mean, then:

- α% of sample means (each based on n observations) will lie within z^{α} standard errors of the population mean.
- The probability that an individual sample mean will lie within z^{α} standard errors of the population mean is α.
- The probability that the population mean will lie within z^{α} standard errors of the sample mean is also α.
- It can be stated with α% confidence that the population mean will be no more than z^{α} standard errors away from the sample mean.

Although it may not be immediately obvious, the above statements are all true.

For a continuous measure with a Normal distribution: large samples

The α% confidence interval for the population mean μ is given by:

$$\text{sample mean} - (z^{\alpha}.SEM) < \mu < \text{sample mean} + (z^{\alpha}.SEM)$$

or, more conventionally, by:

$$\text{sample mean} \pm z^{\alpha}.SEM$$

This is all a bit mathematical. It might help at this point to look at some specific examples. The z^{α} values for the most commonly quoted confidence intervals are given in the table below.

Interval width	50%	75%	90%	95%	99%
z^{α}	0.675	1.150	1.645	1.960	2.576

So the 90% confidence interval for the population mean μ is given by:

$$\text{sample mean} \pm 1.645\,.\,SEM$$

And the 95% confidence interval for the population mean μ is given by:

$$\text{sample mean} \pm 1.960\,.\,SEM$$

and so on ... Clearly, as the level of confidence needed increases:

- the value of z^{α} increases, and
- the width of the confidence interval increases.

The above formulae hold for large samples (and if the population variance is known exactly). When there are only a small number of observations, however, the sample means tend to follow a Student t-distribution (see Chapter 4, Section 4.6). Thus, this distribution must be used for small samples.

For a continuous measure with a Normal distribution: small samples

The α% confidence interval for the population mean μ is given by:

$$\text{sample mean} - (t_{(1-\alpha, n-1)}\,.\,SEM) < \mu < \text{sample mean} + (t_{(1-\alpha, n-1)}\,.\,SEM)$$

or, more conventionally, by:

$$\text{sample mean} \pm t_{(1-\alpha, n-1)}\,.\,SEM$$

Now, the multiplication term is $\boldsymbol{t}_{(1-\alpha, n-1)}$. This is the (1 – α)% value of the Student *t*-distribution with (*n* – 1) degrees of freedom. As usual, *n* denotes the sample size.

Because of the way in which most tables of the *t*-distribution are constructed, the (1 – α)% value has to be used to compute a α% confidence interval. So, for example, the 5% *t*-distribution value has to used to compute a 95% confidence interval.

> It can be stated with α% certainty that the true population mean lies within the α% confidence interval.

Intervals can be constructed for any level of confidence desired.

- The most frequently reported confidence interval is the 95% confidence interval
- It can be stated with 95% certainty that the population mean lies within this interval
- For large samples, *approximate 95% confidence intervals* can be easily computed as:
  - sample mean ± 1.96. SEM
- In many practical situations, this can be simplified even further to:
  - sample mean ± 2. SEM

> For a given level of confidence:
>
> - a narrow interval indicates that the sample estimate has good (= high) precision
> - a wide interval indicates that the sample estimate has poor (= low) precision.

Confidence intervals become narrower (ie the precision of the sample estimate improves) as:

- the sample size increases (as this reduces the value of the standard error)
- the variability of the data decreases (as this also reduces the value of the standard error)
- the degree of confidence required for the population mean decreases (as this reduces the value of the multiplication factor).

The obvious question now is: For what sample sizes is it appropriate to use z and t? The Student t-distribution *must* be used for small samples.

Either the standard normal or Student t-distribution can be used for large samples as the two are effectively indistinguishable.

FOR ALL PRACTICAL PURPOSES THEREFORE: THE STUDENT *T*-DISTRIBUTION SHOULD ALWAYS BE USED TO CALCULATE CONFIDENCE INTERVALS FROM SAMPLES.

Confidence intervals are particularly informative when computed for differences between means. These indicate the likely limits for the true difference between the means (ie the likely range for true difference in the efficacies of the treatments being compared).

Example

A group of 400 patients with hypertension were treated with a new drug. The mean reduction in DBP was 12 mmHg, with a standard error of 4. Thus, we can be 95% certain that the average effect of this drug for the whole population of hypertensive patients lies in the range:

$$12 \pm (1.96 \times 4) = 12 \pm 8 = 4\text{–}20 \text{ mmHg}$$

7.3.2 Confidence intervals for a binomial distribution (qualitative data)

The principles described above for quantitative measures hold also for qualitative data. Only the process of calculating confidence intervals differs. For a categorical (qualitative) measure, the α% confidence interval for the proportion of patients in a sample of size n with a particular characteristic (eg whose ulcer was 'healed') is computed as follows.

Small samples

Exactly from the mathematical properties of the binomial distribution.

Large samples

Using the approximation of the binomial distribution to the Normal distribution (see Chapter 4, Section 4.4). If the proportion of individuals in a random sample of size n with a particular characteristic is $\boldsymbol{p}$ then the α% confidence limits for the true population proportion of individuals (**P**) with the characteristic is computed by:

$$p \pm (t_{(1-\alpha, n-1)} . \sqrt{[p . (1-p)/n]})$$

Example

In the group of 400 patients with hypertension treated with a new drug, 40 (10%) experienced a mild side-effect. Thus, we can be 95% certain that the true population toxicity risk for the whole population of hypertensive patients lies in the range:

$$0.10 \pm (1.96 . \sqrt{[0.10 . 0.90/400]}) = 0.10 \pm (1.96 . 0.015) = 0.10 \pm 0.03$$

ie 0.07 to 0.13 (7% to 13%).

7.4 Reference ranges

Confidence limits allows statements to be made about the likely range of values within which a population value such as a mean or proportion lies. In many clinical situations, it is more important to know the range of values within which it is likely that the observation from an individual patient will lie. Such intervals are called *reference* (or normal) *ranges*. These are computed using the same formulae as shown in Section 7.3, but with the standard error replaced by the standard deviation.

A good example of reference ranges used in clinical practice are provided by the tables of normal values for lung function tests.

8 Significance tests

8.1 Basic principles

In a simple clinical trial, hypertensive patients were randomly allocated to receive either of two drugs to reduce their blood pressure.

Suppose there is strong evidence suggesting that one drug is more effective than the other. When the study results are analysed, we would expect to find a difference in the mean reduction of blood pressure with the two drugs.

But suppose, however, that the two drugs actually have identical therapeutic effects. Now we would expect the mean changes in blood pressure to be exactly the same for both drugs. In reality, however, this is very unlikely to happen.

As the patients allocated to each treatment are random samples from the population of patients with hypertension, the mean reduction in blood pressure observed in each group will be the *estimate* of the true effect of that drug, and it will be subject to sampling error. This error will be slightly different in both groups. So, even when the two drugs are equally effective, the most likely outcome of the study is that the observed changes in blood pressure will be different.

> Even in a well designed and conducted randomised clinical trial:
>
> - if the effects of the treatments being compared are *different*, we can expect to observe a difference
> - if the effects of the treatments being compared are *identical*, we can expect to observe a difference.

This presents a major dilemma. The clinical trial will have been carried out because it is not known whether the treatments have similar or different effects.

How can it be determined whether the difference in estimated effects observed between the treatments:

- was due to a real difference in their therapeutic effects (ie was systematic variation), or
- was just the result of chance (ie random variation)?

This rather intractable problem can be tackled using an appropriate **significance test** (or **hypothesis test**).

8.2 Hypotheses and *P*-values

Significance tests are used to decide which of two (mutually exclusive and exhaustive) hypotheses should be accepted on the basis of the observations collected in the study. These hypotheses always have the same basic format.

Null hypothesis: This is usually a statement of *no difference*, eg:

- the true therapeutic effects of the two drugs are identical
- the true difference in the effects of the treatments is zero

Alternative hypothesis: This is usually a statement of *actual difference*, eg:

- the true therapeutic effects of the two drugs are different
- the true difference in the effects of the treatments is not zero.

Alternative hypotheses have two different forms.

- **Two-sided alternative**: the direction of the difference is not stated in advance. The study is conducted with an open mind. The therapeutic effects of the treatments are believed to differ, but the difference could be in either direction.
- **One-sided alternative**: the direction of the difference *is* stated in advance. The study is conducted with a closed mind, in the sense that the treatments are believed to differ in a specific direction.

Conventionally, significance tests should be two-sided wherever possible. However, there may be situations in which a one-sided alternative might be appropriate (eg if the new treatment is much more expensive or toxic than the standard treatment, so will only be used clinically if it has a clear therapeutic advantage).

8.3 *P*-values

Having stated appropriate null and alternative hypotheses, the next step is to conduct an properly designed trial. The observations from the study are then analysed using appropriate significance tests. These are described below in Sections 8.8 and 8.9.

All significance tests produce a **test statistic**, which is then converted into a *P*-value. As *P*-values are often very poorly understood and interpreted incorrectly, it is worth considering these in detail.

> The ***P*-value** produced by a test statistic is usually stated in either of the following ways:
>
> - the probability that the difference observed in the study (or one more extreme) could have occurred if the null hypothesis is true
> - the probability that the observed difference or one more extreme could have occurred by chance.

Strictly, as *P*-values are used in situations other than comparative trials, a more general definition of a *P*-value is: the probability that the observations produced in the study could have occurred if the Null hypothesis is true.

Clearly:

- as the *P*-value becomes smaller, the difference observed becomes less and less compatible with the null hypothesis;
- a point must be reached eventually where the *P*-value becomes so small that the decision has to be taken that the study data can no longer be accepted as supporting the null hypothesis.

The *P*-value level at which this decision is taken is called the **significance level** (or **critical level**). When *p* falls below this level:

- the observed difference is so unlikely to have occurred by chance that the null hypothesis must be rejected and the alternative hypothesis (of a real difference) accepted
- the observed difference between the treatments is said to be **statistically significant**.

> Conventionally, statistical significance is usually set at 5% ($p = 0.05$).

Thus, the null hypothesis is rejected if there is less than a 5% chance that the observed difference could have occurred if this hypothesis is true.

The choice of a significance level is actually arbitrary. Any value can be used. The 5% level just happens to be used more than any other.

As the actual *P*-value is produced by all good statistical computer packages, it is becoming increasingly common to quote this exactly.

Setting the critical level of *p* as low as 5% may seem extreme. The testing of hypotheses, however, is analogous to the process of trial by jury. Jurors are directed by a judge to return a guilty verdict only if the weight of evidence is against the defendant; similarly, researchers are required to reject the null hypothesis of no difference only if the weight of evidence (the balance of probabilities) from the clinical study is overwhelmingly against it.

8.4 Type I and type II errors

Significance tests are prone to two types of error, ie there are two situations in which the *P*-value can lead to an erroneous conclusion.

	True situation	
	Null hypothesis true	Null hypothesis false
Conclusion from test statistic		
Null hypothesis true	*Correct*	Type II error (β)
Null hypothesis false	Type I error (α)	*Correct*

Types of error possible with test statistics

A **type I error** (false-positive result) occurs if the null hypothesis is rejected when it is actually true (the treatments are interpreted as having different effects when they do not). The probability of committing a type I error (α) is often similar to, *but is not equal to*, the *P*-value.

Using the conventional 5% significance level, a significant difference will occur purely by chance once in every 20 tests performed on average (even though no difference exists). One way of minimising the risk of a type I error is to reject the null hypothesis only if the *P*-value is extremely low (eg $p < 0.001$, or even $p < 0.0001$).

A **type II error** (false-negative result) occurs if the null hypothesis is accepted when it is actually false (the treatments are interpreted as having equal effects when they are actually different). The probability of committing a type II error is often denoted by β.

8.5 Clinical vs statistical significance

Clinical significance is:

- the smallest therapeutic effect of a treatment that is considered to be clinically valuable
- the smallest difference between the therapeutic effects of two treatments that is considered to be clinically important.

The magnitude and clinical importance of any effect found to be statistically significant in a clinical trial must be taken into account when interpreting the result.

- A superior pharmacological effect may be found for drug A than for drug B, but if the side-effect profile or tolerability for drug A is very poor, it may actually be clinically inferior to drug B.
- A small therapeutic effect of a drug may emerge as statistically significant but may be clinically unimportant.
- A clinically significant difference may exist between the treatments, but the study failed to detect it.

If a difference is statistically significant, this does not necessarily make it clinically significant. If a difference is (numerically) clinically significant but not statistically significant, it has an unacceptably high probability of having occurred by chance, so cannot be interpreted as being clinically significant.

STATISTICAL SIGNIFICANCE ≠ CLINICAL SIGNIFICANCE.

8.6 Sample size and statistical power

A vital element of any study design is to ensure that it has adequate **power**.

Statistical power is defined as the probability that, if a clinically significant difference exists between the treatments, the study will detect this and establish it as being statistically significant.

Mathematically, power is the inverse of type II error:

$$\text{power} = 1 - \beta$$

If a study is stated as having 80% power, it has a 80% chance of detecting a clinically significant difference between the treatments (if such a difference actually exists).

When a study fails to detect a clinically significant difference between treatments (ie it is found to have inadequate power), this is usually because the sample size used was too small.

Proper consideration must be given to determining the sample size needed to ensure that a study has adequate power. Indeed, summaries of these calculations are increasingly being demanded in papers submitted to medical journals/conferences.

Four mathematically inter-related factors affect the number of patients which must be recruited to the study (**sample size**):

- The level considered acceptable for the type I error rate (usually set at 5%)
- The level considered acceptable for the type II error rate (usually set at either 10% or 20%, corresponding to power levels of 90% and 80%, respectively)

- The difference between the effects of the treatments considered to be *clinically* significant
- The variation in the primary (main) outcome measure.

Reducing the type I error rate, the type II error rate and/or the size of the clinically significant difference in treatment effects increases the number of patients required, as does increasing the size of the experimental error associated with the outcome measure.

Formulae exist, which determine the relationship between these measures and sample size for most experimental situations. These are now incorporated in widely available tables and computer programs.

8.7 General form of test statistics

Test statistics derived for quantitative observations that can be assumed to have a Normal distribution and (large samples of) qualitative observations that can be approximated to a Normal distribution have the same basic form. The primary outcome statistic will usually be:

- the mean difference between the treatment effects

or

- the difference in the proportion of patients responding to a treatment.

This statistic has a theoretical Normal distribution with, under the constraint of the null hypothesis, a mean equal to the hypothesised value (usually **zero**) and a known or estimated variance. The primary outcome statistic is converted into a test statistic with a standard Normal distribution.

> **Test statistic** = (observed effect – hypothesised value)/standard error of observed effect.
>
> In most clinical trials comparing two treatments, the null hypothesis is that the difference in effects is zero, so this test statistic reduces to:
>
> Test statistic = mean (observed) difference/standard error of (observed) difference

This ratio actually measures how far the observed difference is away from the hypothesised value (as stated, usually zero), measured in standard errors. So:

- if the test statistic = 2, the observed difference was two standard errors away from the hypothesised difference
- if the test statistic = 0.75, the observed difference was 0.75 standard errors away from the hypothesised difference
- if the test statistic = z, the observed difference was z standard errors away from the hypothesised difference.

The probability of finding an observation a distance z (or more) from the mean of a Normal distribution can be computed simply from the properties of this distribution (see Chapter 4, Section 4.4). This value is the probability of obtaining the observed difference (or a greater one) when the null hypothesis is true (ie is the *P*-value).

Test statistics have no real intuitive value in their own right. They merely provide a means to an end, being just a transition stage in obtaining the *P*-value.

The following sections describe the general forms of the most commonly used significance tests in randomised clinical trials. Unavoidably, the presentations are quite mathematical. If you find this a problem, it is probably sufficient to concentrate on remembering which tests should be used in particular situations. There are plenty of statistical computer programs around that will take care of the calculations for you.

8.8 Significance tests for qualitative data

8.8.1 Single sample

A clinician has audited his 'heal' rate for the last 100 patients he has treated for ulcerative colitis with drug A. It is 72%. The heal rate claimed by the drug manufacturer is 80%. Is this difference just due to sampling variation, or does the clinician have a local population of patients with particularly persistent disease?

This is resolved using the **binomial test,** which uses the mathematical properties of the binomial distribution to compute the probability of achieving 72 (or fewer) healed patients in a (random) sample of 100 if the true heal rate is 0.80.

8.8.2 Two or more independent samples

Two drug treatments for ulcerative colitis were compared in a randomised clinical trial. Each patient received either drug A or drug B.

The null hypothesis was that the heal rates are the same for both drugs; the alternative hypothesis was that the heal rates differ (in either direction).

- Of the n_A patients treated with drug A,
  - a were healed and $(n_A - a)$ were not healed
  - so the estimated heal rate for drug A was: $\boldsymbol{p_A = a/n_A}$
- Of the n_B patients treated with drug B,
  - b were healed and $(n_B - b)$ were not healed
  - so the estimated heal rate for drug B was: $\boldsymbol{p_B = b/n_B}$

Both heal rates are proportions with theoretical binomial distributions. If the null hypothesis is true, the two drugs have identical heal rates, so the results for the two drugs can be combined to obtain the best available estimate of (overall) heal rate:

$$\text{Overall heal rate } p = (n_A.p_A + n_B.p_B)/(n_A + n_b) = (a + b)/(n_A + n_B)$$

$$\text{Overall non-heal rate } q = 1 - p$$

The statistical significance of the difference between the heal rates can be determined in two ways.

Using the binomial distribution: small samples

The probability that the observed difference (or one more extreme) could have occurred under the null hypothesis can be computed exactly from the properties of the binomial distribution. This is known as the **Fisher exact test**.

The Fisher test is computationally extremely complex. Most computer programs have algorithms that will attempt the necessary calculations, but these may take a considerable amount of time even when using a high power PC. Thus, the Fisher exact test is best used only for small sample sizes.

Using the binomial distribution: large samples

For large samples, the binomial distribution approximates to a Normal distribution with:

- mean (difference in heal rates) $= p_A - p_B$
- standard error (of difference in heal rates) $= se(p_A - p_B)$ $= \sqrt{[(p \cdot q/n_A) + (p \cdot q/n_B)]}$

Thus, the following test statistic has a standard Normal distribution:

$$z = \text{mean difference in heal rates/standard error of difference in heal rates}$$

$$z = (p_A - p_B)/\sqrt{[(p \cdot q/n_A) + (p \cdot q/n_B)]}$$

The required p-value is obtained by referring the value of z to tables of the standard Normal distribution.

Using the chi-squared (χ^2) test/contingency tables

The results of the ulcerative colitis study discussed above can be summarised in the form of a 2 × 2 contingency table.

For this contingency table the values a, b, c and d are the **observed values** for the cells in the contingency table:

	Treatment		
Outcome	Drug A	Drug B	Total
Healed	a	b	$a + b$
Not healed	$c = (n_A - a)$	$d = (n_B - b)$	$c + d$
Total	$a + c = n_A$	$b + d = n_B$	$a + b + c + d$ $(n_A + n_B)$

- the estimated probability of being healed on drug A $= p_A = a/n_A$ $= a/(a + c)$
- the estimated probability of being healed on drug B $= p_B = b/n_B$ $= b/(b + d)$
- the common (null hypothesis) probability of being healed $= p$ $= (a + b)/(n_A + n_B) = (a + b)/(a + b + c + d)$

The **expected values** for the cells in this contingency table are computed by assuming that the null hypothesis is true. Under this condition, the proportion of patients cured should be $\boldsymbol{p}$ for both drugs (and so the proportion not healed should be $\boldsymbol{q}$ for both drugs). So:

- the expected number of healed patients with drug A = $p \cdot n_A$
- the expected number of unhealed patients with drug A = $q \cdot n_A$
- the expected number of healed patients with drug B = $p \cdot n_B$
- the expected number of unhealed patients with drug B = $q \cdot n_B$

The test statistic for a contingency table is obtained by:

- Computing for each cell in the table the statistic:

  (observed value – expected value)^2/expected value

- Summing the values obtained over all of the cells in the table

The test statistic produced has a theoretical χ^2-distribution with k degrees of freedom. The **degrees of freedom** for a contingency table χ^2-statistic are equal to:

$$k = (\text{number of rows in table} - 1) \times (\text{number of columns in table} - 1)$$

The p-value is obtained by referring the test statistic value obtained to tables of the χ^2-distribution with the appropriate degrees of freedom. The calculation of this χ^2-statistic is based on a number of (fairly dubious) assumptions and approximations. These give rise to several important criteria that restrict the validity of the test.

- The approximations used in the calculations tend to break down when there are just two rows and two columns in the table. In this situation, the Yates continuity correction has to be applied. (The exact nature of this correction is outside the scope of this primer – all good statistical programs recognise when this correction is necessary and apply it automatically.)
- The approximations also tend to break down if any of the expected cell frequencies are 5 or smaller (ie the test is valid only if all expected cell frequencies exceed 5). However, a more relaxed rule is often advocated, which requires 80% of the expected cell frequencies to exceed 5 and for all of them to exceed 1.

- Contingency table analyses are valid only if *a*, *b*, *c* and *d* are actual numbers of patients; converting the numbers to percentages totally invalidates the test statistic.
- The χ^2 test should really only be used when the Fisher exact test cannot be computed.

8.8.3 Dependent samples

In a simple audit exercise, two radiologists rate the same series of breast X-ray plates, to diagnose whether there is evidence of cancer. The ratings produced by the two radiologists are *not* independent – the ratings have to be paired to determine the extent to which they agree on a diagnosis.

The usual summary statistic in this situation is **percentage agreement**. However, the **Kappa statistic** should also be considered, as this adjusts for random agreement (if the radiologists were simply guessing, they would still agree some of the time by chance). Arguably, if the agreement statistic is unacceptably low clinically, no further analysis is necessary. The radiologists need to work out why this is so.

If the agreement level is acceptably high, the null hypothesis that the two radiologists agree (ie that any disagreements are random) can be tested against the alternative hypothesis that the disagreements are consistently in one direction (ie one radiologist tends to over or under diagnoses cancers) using the **McNemar test**.

The McNemar test uses only the pairs of observations that disagree. So, if there is agreement on 98% of the plates, only the 2% where there was a disagreement contribute to the test. The McNemar test then simply reduces to the binomial test. The number of instances in which radiologist 1 diagnosed a cancer and radiologist 2 did not is compared with the number of instances in which the disagreement was the other way round.

The probability of obtaining these two numbers if both types of disagreement are equally likely is calculated from the mathematical properties of the binomial distribution.

This test can be extended to three or more repeated tests/ratings using the **Cochran Q-test**.

8.8.4 Number needed to treat

A clinically useful measure of the efficacy of a new treatment is **number needed to treat** (**NNT**).

> **NNT**: is the number of patients who have to be prescribed the new treatment to either:
>
> - prevent one extra person from having an adverse event
>
> or
>
> - enable one extra person to have a successful outcome
>
> relative to the comparison (control) treatment.

NNT is the inverse of the risk difference. For the ulcerative colitis discussed study above:

- the '**risk**' of not being healed on drug A = $a/n_A = a/(a + c) = r_A$
- the '**risk**' of not being healed on drug B = $b/n_B = b/(b + d) = r_B$
- the **relative risk/risk ratio** for drug A relative to drug B = r_A/r_B
- the **risk difference** for drug A relative to drug B = $r_A - r_B$
- number needed to treat = NNT = $1/(r_A - r_B)$
  (*If* $r_A - r_B$ is negative, the minus sign is ignored.)

8.8.5 Worked example

If all of the algebra and mathematical notation in the previous sections have left you perplexed and even more confused than when you started, the following worked example may help. The actual results of the ulcerative colitis study above were as follows.

	Treatment		
Outcome	Drug A	Drug B	Total
Healed	81	88	169
Not healed	41	30	71
Total	122	118	240

- The **estimated probability** of being healed on drug A = p_A = 81/122 = 0.664
- The **estimated probability** of being healed on drug B = p_B = 88/118 = 0.746
- The **common (null hypothesis) probability** of being healed = p = 169/240 = 0.704

The expected values for the cell in this contingency table are computed by assuming that the null hypothesis is true. Under this condition, the proportion of patients cured should be ***p*** for both drugs (and so the proportion not healed should be ***q*** for both drugs). So:

- the **expected number** of healed patients with drug A = $p.\ n_A$ = 0.704 . 122 = 85.9
- the **expected number** of unhealed patients with drug A = $q.\ n_A$ = 0.296 . 122 = 36.1
- the **expected number** of healed patients with drug B = $p\ .\ n_B$ = 0.704 . 118 = 83.1
- the **expected number** of unhealed patients with drug B = $q\ .\ n_B$ = 0.296 . 118 = 34.9
- the '**risk**' of being healed on drug A = 0.664
- the '**risk**' of being healed on drug B = 0.746
- the **relative risk/risk ratio** for drug B relative to drug A = 0.746/0.664 = 1.123
  ie Patients treated with drug B are 1.123 times more likely to be treated than those treated with drug A.
- the **risk difference** for drug A relative to drug B = 0.336 – 0.254 = 0.082
- Number needed to treat = **NNT** = 1/0.082 = 12.2 = 13 (rounded up to nearest integer).

We need to treat 13 patients with drug B to achieve one extra patient being healed compared to drug A.

8.9 Significance tests for quantitative (continuous) data

8.9.1 Parametric and non-parametric methods

Difference types of significance test have to be used for continuous measures, depending on whether the measures have a Normal distribution. The tests are often classified as **parametric** and **non-parametric** tests.

As their name suggests, non-parametric/distribution-free methods make no assumption about the nature of the underlying data distribution. Parametric statistical methods, conversely, assume a specific distribution for the observations and use the mathematical properties of that distribution.

When a continuous variable can be assumed to follow a Normal distribution:

- parametric statistical significance tests are used to compare treatment effects
- the appropriate summary statistics in this situation are means, standard deviations and standard errors.

When a continuous variable cannot be assumed to follow a Normal distribution:

- attempts should be made to transform the observations into a Normal distribution
- if a Normalising transformation cannot be found, and the data do not follow any other recognisable distribution, non-parametric statistical methods are used to compare treatment effects
- the appropriate summary statistics in this situation are medians and ranges.

Non-parametric methods usually involve ranking the original observations into ascending order and then replacing these with their rank scores. The test statistics are computed using the rank scores. These methods throw away a lot of information – so are less powerful (ie are less likely to detect statistically significant differences) than parametric methods. They should be used only when it would clearly be inappropriate to assume a Normal distribution for the observations.

8.9.2 Single samples

In a simple observational study, blood glucose levels were measured in a single group of n individuals before and after a glucose challenge test. The test was expected to increase blood glucose levels by an average of X g/dl. If the observations can be assumed to follow a Normal distribution:

- The **Student one-sample *t*-test** should be used to evaluate whether the mean change (in blood glucose level) is equal to or different from the hypothesised change X
- Under the null hypothesis that the means are equal, the test statistic takes the form:

  t = (observed mean change – X)/(standard error of observed mean change)

- This has a Student t-distribution with $(n - 1)$ degrees of freedom (ie the total number of observations minus the number of mean values calculated).
- The P-value is obtained by referring the test statistic value to tables of the t-distribution with $(n - 1)$ degrees of freedom.

8.9.3 Two independent samples

> Observations collected from distinct groups of individuals constitute **independent** samples.

In a simple randomised controlled trial, blood glucose levels were measured in two different groups of individuals:

- The n_1 subjects in group 1 were allocated to a normal diet.
- The n_2 subjects in group 2 were allocated a diet with a high sugar content.

Changes in blood glucose levels were measured in all patients at the end of the study period. If the observations can be assumed to follow a Normal distribution:

- The **Student independent samples/unpaired *t*-test** should be used to evaluate the difference (in mean blood glucose level change) between two groups.

- Under the null hypothesis that the means are equal, the test statistic takes the form:

  t = (mean for group 1 – mean for group 2)/(standard error of difference in means)

- This has a Student t-distribution with $(n_1 + n_2 - 2)$ degrees of freedom (ie the total number of observations minus the number of mean values calculated).
- The P-value is obtained by referring the test statistic value to tables of the t-distribution with $(n_1 + n_2 - 2)$ degrees of freedom.

Mathematically, this t-test is valid only if the variances of the observations are equal in both groups. The equality of the sample variances can be tested using the Levene test as follows:

- Compute the variance estimates for the two samples (s_1^2 and s_2^2).
- Compute the ratio of the larger variance estimate (s_1^2) to the smaller variance estimate (s_2^2).
- Under the Null hypothesis that the two variances are equal, this ratio (s_1^2/s_2^2) has a theoretical F-distribution with $(n_1 - 1)$ and $(n_2 - 1)$ degrees of freedom.
- The p-value is obtained by referring the test statistic value to Tables of the F-distribution with $(n_1 - 1)$ and $(n_2 - 1)$ degrees of freedom.

If the variances of the two samples are *equal*, the test is straightforward. The two estimated sample variances are pooled and this value is used to compute the test statistic.

If the variances of the two samples are *not equal*, the test is technically invalid. However, an approximate t-test statistic can be computed using the separate variance estimates from the two samples and adjusting the degrees of freedom.

If the observations *cannot* be assumed to follow a Normal distribution:

- The **Mann-Whitney U-test** is used to compare the distributions (and hence the difference in the median blood glucose level change) between two groups.
- This test is the non-parametric equivalent of the Student independent samples/unpaired t-test.

- For *small samples*, tables exist which convert the test statistic U into the required *P*-value.
- For *large samples*, U is converted into a *z*-statistic and the *P*-value is determined by reference to the tables of the standard Normal distribution.

8.9.4 Two dependent samples

Observations collected from the same group of individuals on two separate occasions (a within-group comparison) constitute **dependent/paired** samples.

In a simple randomised clinical trial, blood glucose levels were measured in a single group of *n* individuals both before and after a meal with a high sugar content. If the observations can be assumed to follow a Normal distribution:

- The **Student dependent samples/paired *t*-test** is used to evaluate the difference (in mean blood glucose level change) between the pre- and post-meal observations.
- The test statistic is computed by taking the difference between the two blood levels for each individual separately and then calculating the mean of these differences.
- Under the null hypothesis that the means are equal, the test statistic takes the form:

$$t = (\text{mean difference})/(\text{standard error of mean difference})$$

- This has a Student *t*-distribution with $(n - 1)$ degrees of freedom (ie the total number of *pairs* of observations minus the number of mean values calculated).
- The *P*-value is obtained by referring the test statistic value to tables of the *t*-distribution with $(n - 1)$ degrees of freedom.

If the observations *cannot* be assumed to follow a Normal distribution:

- The **Wilcoxon matched pairs rank-sum test** is used to compare the distributions (and hence the difference in the median blood glucose levels) on the two occasions.
- This test is the non-parametric equivalent of the Student dependent samples/paired *t*-test.

- For *small samples*, tables exist which convert the test statistic T into the required P-value.
- For *large samples*, T is converted into a z-statistic and the P-value is determined by reference to the tables of the standard Normal distribution.

8.9.5 More than two samples

Independent samples

When there are three or more independent groups, these can be compared in pairs using either unpaired t-tests or Mann–Whitney U-tests as appropriate. However, the number of comparisons needed is very large if there are many groups to be compared – so the risk of a type I error increases rapidly.

If the measure can be assumed to have a Normal distribution, the groups can all be compared simultaneously using a one-way analysis of variance (**one-way ANOVA**). This produces an F-statistic, which tests the null hypothesis that the means are equal for all of the groups, against the alternative that the means are not all equal. If this test is significant, appropriate post-hoc **multiple comparison tests** need to be applied to identify exactly where the differences are.

If the measure cannot be assumed to have a Normal distribution, the non-parametric equivalent of the one-way ANOVA is used, called the **Kruskal–Wallis test**.

Independent samples

When the same group of individuals is assessed on three or more occasions, the assessment times can be compared in pairs using either paired t-tests or Wilcoxon matched pairs rank-sum tests as appropriate. Again, however, the number of comparisons needed is very large if there are many groups to be compared – so the risk of a type I error increases rapidly.

If the measure can be assumed to have a Normal distribution, the assessment times can all be compared simultaneously using a **repeated measures analysis of variance (ANOVA)**. This is very similar to the one-way ANOVA, but is computed very differently. The test again produces an F-statistic, which tests the null hypothesis that the means are equal at all of the assessment times, against the alternative that the means are not all equal. If this test is significant, appropriate post-hoc **multiple comparison tests** need to be applied to identify exactly where the differences are.

If the measure cannot be assumed to have a Normal distribution, the non-parametric equivalent of the repeated measures ANOVA is used, called the **Friedman test**.

8.10 Summary

The scientific process for conducting a comparative study takes the following general form:

- State appropriate null and alternative hypotheses.
- Carry out an appropriately designed study.
- Select and compute appropriate statistical significance tests.
- Convert the test statistics results into p-values.
- Accept either the null or the alternative hypothesis.

9 Significance tests or confidence intervals

CONFIDENCE INTERVALS SHOULD ALWAYS BE USED IN PREFERENCE TO SIGNIFICANCE TESTS WHENEVER POSSIBLE.

In general terms, confidence intervals are more informative than significance tests.

In fact, confidence intervals provide essentially the same information as a significance test – plus a lot more besides.

The reason for this is simple. In many situations, and certainly if the observations either have a Normal distribution or can (for a large sample) be approximated to this distribution, confidence intervals and significance tests are mathematically identical.

The advantages of confidence intervals over significance tests are best illustrated by a practical example.

Example

The difference in the mean blood glucose levels of two (different/independent) groups of individuals receiving either a normal or a high sugar content diet was 2.3 mmol/l.

Situation 1: the 95% confidence interval for this difference is +0.7 to +3.9 mmol/l.

On the basis of this confidence interval, we can conclude, with 95% certainty, that the true mean glucose level in individuals with a high sugar diet is between 0.7 mmol/1 and 3.9 mmol/1 higher than that in individuals with a normal diet. Clearly, being on a high sugar content diet increases blood glucose levels. However, our estimate of exactly how great this increase is on average is not particularly precise.

Importantly, this 95% confidence interval does *not* include the value zero.

If we adopt a significance test to the result of this study, the null hypothesis would be that blood glucose levels are the same on both diets (ie the difference in mean blood glucose levels for the two diets is zero). But, clearly, the 95% confidence interval does not support zero as a likely difference in mean blood glucose levels.

In this instance, the mathematical formulae for the confidence interval and significance test are identical. So, we can conclude that the null hypothesis value is not supported by the 95% confidence interval. Hence we must reject the null hypothesis and accept the alternative hypothesis.

In this situation, the difference in mean blood glucose levels is statistically significant (at the 5% level).

Situation 2: the 95% confidence interval for this difference is – 0.7 to +5.3 mmol/l.

On the basis of this confidence interval, we can conclude, with 95% certainty, that true mean glucose level in individuals with a high sugar diet is between 0.7 mmol/1 *lower* and 5.3 mmol/1 *higher* than that in individuals with a normal diet. The consequence to blood glucose levels of being on a high sugar content diet is unclear. One end of the interval suggests that levels are reduced, while the other end suggest they are raised. *Importantly*, this 95% confidence interval *does* now include the value zero.

If we adopt a significance test to the result of this study, the null hypothesis would again be that blood glucose levels are the same on both diets (ie the difference in mean blood glucose levels for the two diets is zero). This 95% confidence interval supports zero as a likely difference in mean blood glucose levels.

As before, the mathematical formulae for the confidence interval and significance test are identical. So, we can conclude that the null hypothesis value *is* supported by the 95% confidence interval. Hence we must accept the null hypothesis and reject the alternative hypothesis.

In this situation, the difference in mean blood glucose levels is *not* statistically significant (at the 5% level).

However, before we can conclude that there is no evidence that a high sugar content diet affects blood glucose levels, we must also consider clinical significance. Suppose blood glucose levels have to differ by 6.0 mmol/l or more to be considered clinically significant. In this instance, the 95% confidence interval shows that the difference:

- was not statistically significant
- was also not clinically significant as neither limit of the interval reaches 6.0 mmol/l.

We can, with some confidence, conclude that a high sugar content diet is not harmful (at least as measured by blood glucose levels).

But now suppose blood glucose levels have to differ by just 3.0 mmol/l or more to be considered clinically significant. In this instance, the 95% confidence interval shows that the difference:

- was not statistically significant
- but cannot exclude the possibility that the difference is clinically significant as the upper limit of the interval exceeds 3.0 mmol/l.

Now, the study failed to find evidence to an acceptably high statistical level that blood glucose levels are systematically changed, but the possibility remains that clinically significant changes do occur on average. There is a very real possibility that the result of this study is a type II (false negative) finding. No conclusion can be drawn with any confidence from it.

- If the confidence interval for a difference does *not* include the null hypothesis value (usually zero), the difference is statistically significant.
- If the confidence interval for a difference *does* include the null hypothesis value (usually zero), the difference is not statistically significant.
- If a difference is not *statistically* significant but the confidence interval includes values that constitute a *clinically* significant difference, the study findings cannot be easily interpreted.
- A α% confidence interval is equivalent to a (100 – α%) significance test, ie a 95% confidence interval is equivalent to a 5% significance test.

10 Measures of association

10.1 Scatterplots

> Before calculating statistics to measure the strength of any relationship between two variables (measures), it is essential to initially assess the likely nature of this relationship graphically.

The most effective way of assessing the nature of any association between two variables is by constructing a **scatterplot**.

Example

Levels of anxiety and depression were measured in a group of 15 patients with diabetes. A scatterplot of the study observations (Figure 12) shows evidence of:

- a *definite* but weak relationship, with high levels of depression tending to be associated with high levels of anxiety (and vice versa)
- a *linear* relationship – the levels of depression appear to increase at a constant rate as the levels of anxiety increase.

For a scatterplot drawn solely to examine the general nature of the relationship, it is irrelevant which variable is plotted on the vertical axis and which variable is plotted on the horizontal axis. In many situations, however, there is an underlying belief that the relationship is **causal**, in that the level of one of the variables affects the level of the other (either directly or indirectly).

For example, the relationship between body mass index (BMI) and the dose of anaesthetic is causal, ie the dose of anaesthetic required by a patient depends on their BMI – in general, patients with higher BMI require larger doses of anaesthetic. The nature of this relationship

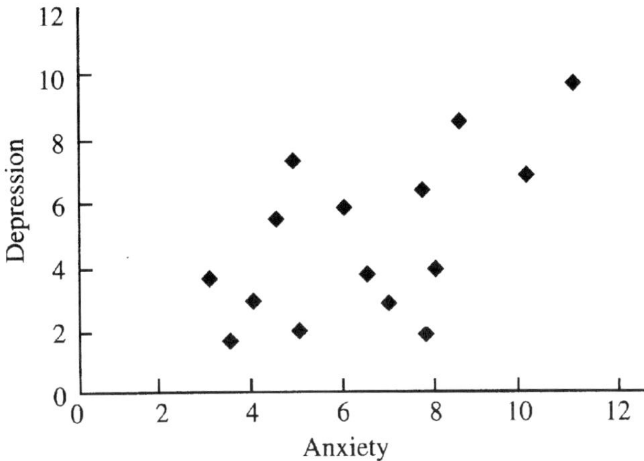

Figure 12 Scatter plot suggesting an association between anxiety and depression

should help us to estimate the dose of anaesthetic needed for a patient with a particular BMI. In this situation:

- the dose of anaesthetic is the **dependent (outcome/predicted/response)** variable
- the BMI is the **independent (predictor)** variable.

If the relationship is thought to be causal, the scatterplot should be constructed as follows:

- the outcome/dependent variable is plotted on the vertical (y) axis
- the predictor/independent variable is plotted on the horizontal (x) axis.

10.2 Correlation

> A **correlation coefficient** measures the strength of the relationship between two variables.

If a scatterplot suggests that two variables may be (mathematically) related, a correlation coefficient can be computed.

Correlation coefficients have a number of important properties:

- Correlations only take values in the range – 1 to +1 inclusive.
- A positive correlation value (ie in the range 0 to +1) indicates a positive relationship between the two variables (ie as one variable increases, the other also increases).
- A negative correlation value (ie in the range – 1 to 0) indicates a negative relationship between the two variables (ie as one variable increases, the other decreases).
- If the correlation value is equal to +1 or – 1, the two variables are perfectly correlated – all of the observations lie on a perfect straight line (eg Figure 13).
- If the correlation is equal to 0 (zero), there is no association between the two variables (the observations obtained for the two variables are totally unrelated).
- The correlation is often regarded as strong if $r < -0.5$ or $r > +0.5$.
- The correlation is often regarded as weak if $-0.5 \leq r \geq +0.5$.
- Correlation coefficients are dimensionless statistics (ie they have no units).
- Correlation coefficients provide *no* information about the form of

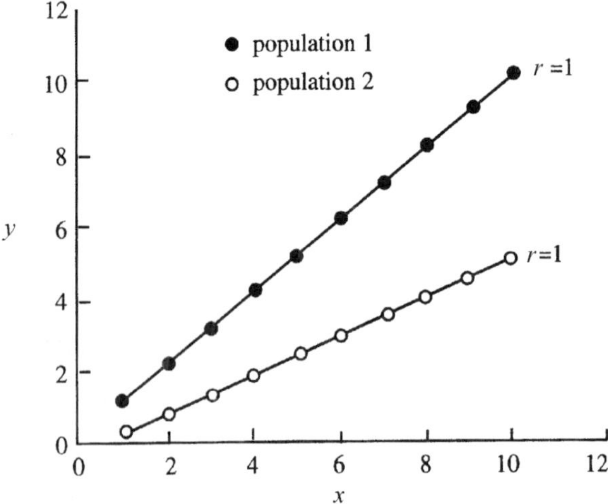

Figure 13 Perfect positive correlations

any relationship – so cannot be used directly to predict the value of one variable from the value of the other

- As the value of the correlation coefficient approaches zero, the association between the two variables becomes weaker (ie the scatter of the points about the line of perfect relationship increases; see Figure 14).

Considerable caution should be exercised when interpreting the significance of a correlation. The *P*-value obtained is dependent both on the strength of the association and, in a sense more importantly, on the sample size. Thus:

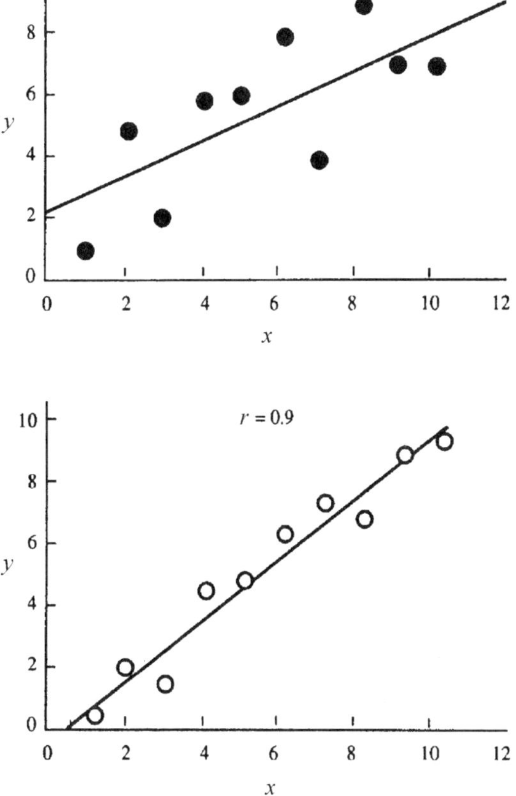

Figure 14 Positive correlations

- a small correlation can be statistically significant if the sample size is very large
- a large correlation can be statistically non-significant if the sample size is small.

A more useful statistic is the **square of the correlation coefficient** (usually denoted by R^2). This is the proportion of the variation in one of the variables accounted for by its relationship with the other.

The R^2 statistic gives a more realistic context in which to interpret the clinical relevance of a correlation coefficient.

Suppose the correlation found between salt intake and blood pressure was statistically significant, with $r = 0.30$. This would seem to indicate that salt intake is a very important factor in determining blood pressure levels.

However, only $(0.30)^2 = 0.09 = 9\%$ of the variation in blood pressure levels is accounted for by the amount of salt in a person's diet. This association has less clinical value than r seemed to suggest. Certainly, the results indicate that salt intake should probably be kept to a minimum, but there are clearly many other factors affecting blood pressure (accounting for the remaining 91% of the variation).

A STATISTICALLY SIGNIFICANT CORRELATION BETWEEN TWO VARIABLES DOES NOT IMPLY THAT THEY ARE CAUSALLY RELATED.

Famously, a significant correlation is reputed to have been found between the number of storks ringed in Norway and the number of babies born in the UK in the early part of the twentieth century. This is clearly not a causal relationship.

10.2.1 Pearson correlation coefficient

The **Pearson correlation coefficient** measures the strength of the relationship between two variables when:

- both variables are continuous
- at least one of the variables can be assumed to have a Normal distribution
- the relationship is linear.

The Pearson correlation coefficient:

- measures how close the relationship between the two measures is to a straight line
- is usually denoted by the letter *r*.

10.2.2 Spearman correlation coefficient

The Pearson correlation coefficient should not be used if:

- the scattergram suggests that the relationship between the variables is not linear
- the relationship *is* linear but the conditions required by the Pearson correlation coefficient do not apply.

Instead, it may be possible to use the Spearman correlation coefficient.

The **Spearman correlation coefficient** also measures the strength of the relationship between two variables. It requires that:

- both variables are continuous or ordinal (ordered categories)
- the relationship between the two variables is merely monotonic (ie as one variable increase, the other variable always increases or always decreases; see Figure 15).

No assumption is required about the distribution of either variable.

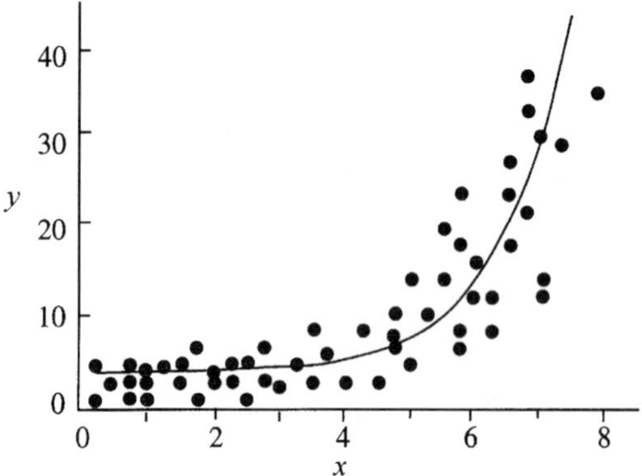

Figure 15 Non-linear (curvilinear) monotonic correlation

The Spearman correlation coefficient has exactly the same properties as those described for the Pearson correlation coefficient (Section 10.2.1). In fact, the two coefficients are calculated using exactly the same mathematical formula, except that:

- the Pearson correlation coefficient is computed using the actual observation values
- the Spearman correlation coefficient is computed using rank scores of the observation values for each variable.

The Spearman correlation coefficient is thus often referred to as being the non-parametric equivalent of the Pearson correlation coefficient.

10.2.3 Complex non-linear relationships

If the scattergram shows that the relationship between two variables changes direction at least once (ie has at least one clear **turning point** – see Figure 16), neither the Pearson nor the Spearman correlation coefficient is valid. Although there may be an obvious association between the variables, both of these coefficients will produce misleading values (in the case of Figure 16, the values will be close to zero). More complex mathematical methods, outside the scope of this primer, are required to assess the strength of such relationships.

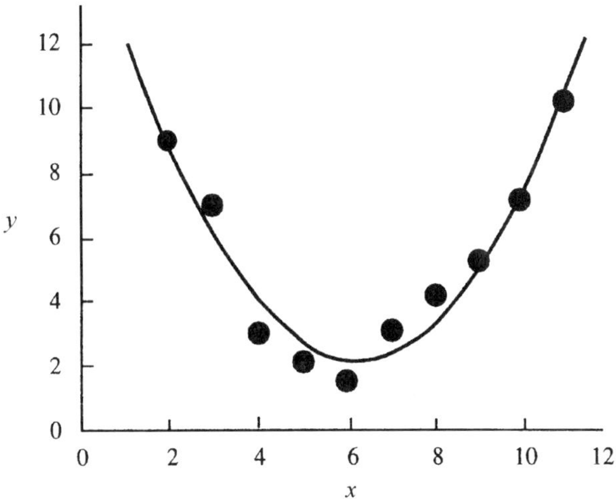

Figure 16 Non-linear non-monotonic correlation

10.2.4 Confidence limits/significance tests for correlations

The Pearson correlation coefficient (r) follows a non-standard distribution, but can be converted to a statistic that has a Normal distribution using the **Fisher z-transformation**:

$$z' = 0.5 \,.\, \ln\,[(1 + r)/(1 - r)]$$

where n is the sample size (number of pairs of observations) and 'ln' denotes the natural logarithm.

This z' statistic is approximately Normally distributed, with mean 0 and standard error $1/\surd\,(n - 3)$.

The α% confidence interval for a Pearson correlation coefficient (r) is computed as follows:

- convert r to a z' statistic
- calculate the α% confidence interval for z':

$$z' \pm [z^{\alpha}/\surd\,(n - 3)]$$

- convert both limits of this interval back to r values by reversing the z' transformation.

(These calculations *are* as complicated as they look! However, there are plenty of free software packages and tables available on the Internet that will do the calculations for you.)

The test statistic for the null hypothesis that the true population correlation is zero is:

$$t = r \,.\, \sqrt{(n-2)} / \sqrt{(1-r^2)}$$

where t is distributed as a student t-distribution with (n–2) degrees of freedom.

10.3 Linear regression

If the scattergram indicates a straight line relationship between two variables, **linear regression** methods can be used to determine the exact mathematical form of the relationship.

Linear regression lines take the form:

$$y = a + b \,.\, x$$

where:

- y is the outcome/dependent variable
- x is the predictor/independent variable
- a is the intercept of the line (this is the value of y when $x = 0$)
- b is the slope of the regression line (this indicates the rate at which y changes ie is the amount y changes when the value of x increases by one unit).

NB The slope of the regression line is *not* equal to the correlation coefficient.

A typical example of a regression line is shown in Figure 17.

Regression lines are frequently used to predict the value of the outcome variable (y) for a known value of the predictor variable (x). This should be done only within the range of values for which the outcome variable has been tested (**interpolation**); estimating values outside this range (**extrapolation**) produces estimates of y which become increasingly unreliable as the distance from the original observations increases.

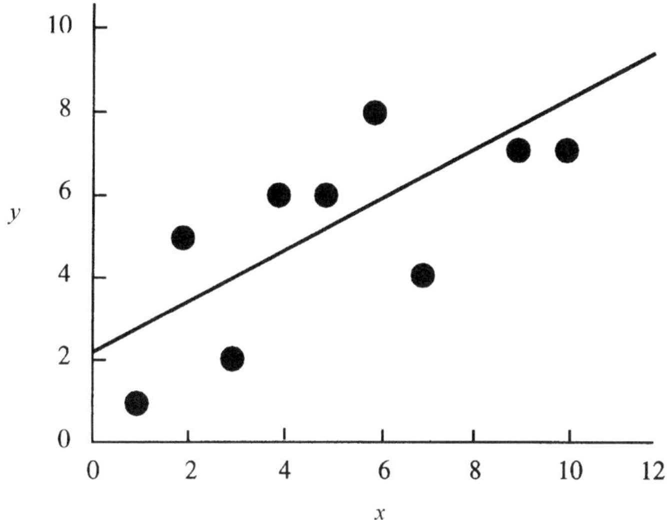

Figure 17 Linear regression line: $y = 2.2 + 0.6x$

Predicted values of y should *always* be presented with their 95% confidence interval, to indicate the precision with which they have been estimated. Significance tests and confidence intervals can be computed for both the intercept and slope of the regression line. The formulae for these are outside the scope of this primer.

Non-linear relationships

If the scattergram indicates that the relationship between two variables is non-linear, a mathematical transformation of one or both variables can often produce a linear relationship.

Suppose two variables are exponentially related (this commonly occurs in biological systems) – taking the natural logarithms of one of the variables should produce a linear relationship.

If no such transformation can be found, non-linear regression methods must be used. These are outside the scope of this primer.

Multiple linear regression

Most biological entities are influenced by more than one factor. Stated in statistical terms, most outcome (dependent) measures in a study are potentially influenced by several independent (predictor) measures.

If the relationship between the outcome variable and several predictor (independent) variables is of interest, multiple linear regression methods can be employed. This produces a mathematical relationship from which the value of the outcome variable (y) is estimated for known values of *several* predictor variables ($x_1, x_2, x_3, ..., x_n$).

Multiple linear regression lines take the form:

$$y = a + b_1.x_1 + b_2.x_2 + b_3.x_3 + \ldots + b_n.x_n$$

Model residuals

There is a widely held misconception that the dependent and independent variables in a (multiple) regression must all be continuous with Normal distributions. This is not true. These can have any distribution.

When the regression model has been fitted, the equation obtained can be used to estimate the *predicted* value of y for each individual in the study. These should all be similar to, but few will be equal to, the actual values of *y observed* for each individual. The differences between the observed and predicted values for each individual are called the model **residuals**.

For the regression model to be considered an acceptable fit to the study observations, these residuals should have a Normal distribution (with mean equal to zero). This can be tested by constructing a histogram of the residuals and testing their distribution as described in Section 4.4.

10.4 Logistic regression

The regression methods described in Section 10.3 assume that the dependent variable (y) is continuous. (They can also be used if y is ordinal, but there are much more powerful methods for this situation that are outside the scope of this primer.)

Commonly, the outcome is a simple dichotomy (typically some form of failure/success). The outcome categories are recorded as 0 and 1.

This is a binary (or Bernoulli) outcome variable. It has a theoretical binomial distribution. Regression analysis models cannot be fitted directly to binary variables. Instead, the outcome measure is based on the *probabilities of each category occurring*. If the probability of success (ie of the 1 category occurring) is p, the probability of failure (ie of the 0 category occurring) is $(1 - p)$.

The odds (ratio) of success is thus (see Chapter 5, Section 5.2):

$$p/(1 - p)$$

Logistic regression methods are used to model these odds ratios.

Logistic regression lines take the form:

$$\ln(p/[1 - p]) = a + b_1.x_1 + b_2.x_2 + b_3.x_3 + \ldots + b_n.x_n$$

The regression coefficients (b_i) are the natural logarithms (ln) of odds ratios. These are thus usually anti-logged (exponentiated) and reported as odds ratios (with their 95% confidence intervals).

10.5 Survival curves/Cox regression

In many studies, particularly in oncology, the outcome measure is length of survival. The analysis of this type of measure is complex, and not just because survival times rarely follow a Normal distribution.

Conventional summary statistics (eg median survival/recovery time) cannot be computed until at least 50% of the patients in the study have died/recovered. This could take many years and render the findings of the study meaningless. The statistical analysis thus has to be carried out before all patients reach the study end-point. So, for many patients we will know only that they had not reached the end-point after some length of time (the time between their entering the study and the study being terminated). The observations for such patients are **censored**.

The results of this type of study are usually summarised using **survival curves** (Figure 18). These plot the proportion of patients who have *not* reached the study end-point over time, with appropriate adjustment for censored data.

There are two widely used methods for drawing survival curves:

- **Actuarial method**: the time axis is divided into intervals and survival calculated for each interval
- **Kaplan–Meier method**: survival is re-calculated every time a patient reaches the end-point.

The Kaplan–Meier method is most widely used. The term **life-table**

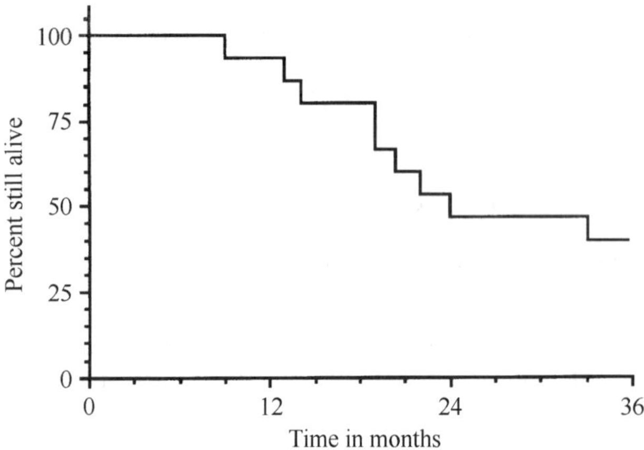

Figure 18 Survival curves

analysis is often applied to both methods.

When comparing survival times for two (or more) treatments, the **log-rank** test is used to test the null hypothesis that there is no difference between the treatments in terms of the probability of an event (death) at any time point.

Cox regression models can be used to determine the influence of predictor variables on survival. These have a very complex form. The outcome measure used is not actual survival time (remember, this will not be known for every patient). Instead, the concept of **hazard rate** is used. **Hazard rate** is computed by dividing the study period into time intervals (usually weeks or months), and then computing for each period the probability that, if a patient has reached the start of a specific period, they will survive to the end of that period.

11 Epidemiology – observational studies

Medical epidemiology is the study of the distribution and the determinants of diseases in human populations. It aims to:

- describe the magnitude of disease occurrence in a population (eg define the incidence and prevalence of illnesses)
- identify the aetiological factors responsible for particular illnesses (generally, this depends on identifying an association between a putative factor and the disease which is being studied)
- provide the information necessary to prevent, control or treat a particular disease in a specific population.

There are two broad groups of epidemiological studies used to address these aims:

- Observational studies: these are described in this chapter.
- Interventional studies (clinical trials): these are described in Chapter 12.

11.1 Observational studies

> **Observational studies** are used to describe the distribution and aetiology of a disease.

Such studies have limited value when attempting to identify possible causative factors, as no controlled intervention can be made to provide definitive evidence of a 'cause-and-effect' relationship. Individuals cannot (usually) be randomly allocated to exposure or non-exposure to a potential health risk factor, so there is no control over who is exposed to the factor and who is not.

Example

The MICA study was carried out in the UK to determine whether women taking the low-dose oral contraceptive pill were at increased risk of coronary heart disease (CHD). It was logistically impossible (and ethically unacceptable) to randomly allocate large numbers of young women to either take or refrain from taking the low-dose oral contraceptive pill. Instead, the study identified a group of young women who had been diagnosed as having CHD and then selected a group of young women with similar characteristics who did not have CHD. The relationship of interest was evaluated by comparing the proportions of low-dose oral contraceptive users in both groups.

THREE major types of observational study will be described:

- Cross-sectional (prevalence) surveys (Section 11.1.1)
- Cohort studies (Section 11.1.2)
- Case–control studies (Section 11.1.3).

11.1.1 Cross-sectional (prevalence) surveys

Cross-sectional (prevalence) surveys simply evaluate and describe a defined population at a specific point in time.

Such surveys are used to estimate for that population the number of people who, at the time of the study:

- have a particular disease

or

- are exposed to a possible aetiological (risk) factor.

A **case** is an individual with the characteristic of interest in the population at a given time.

Prevalence and **incidence** are types of probability used frequently to describe the characteristics of large and/or whole populations. They are usually used to describe the extent of a disease.

Point prevalence: number of cases of the disease known to be in the population at some particular time.

Prevalence rate: (number of cases in population/total size of population) × 100 000

The *total number* of individuals in a population with a particular disease at any given time is the point prevalence for that disease.

The *proportion* of individuals in a population with a particular disease at a given time is the prevalence rate. This is usually expressed as the number of cases per 100 000 individuals in the population and is the probability that any single individual in the population has the disease at a given time.

The total number of *new* individuals in a population diagnosed as having a particular disease in a specific period of time (usually one year) is called the *disease incidence*.

Incidence: number of new cases of the disease diagnosed in the population per unit of time

Incidence rate: (number of new cases diagnosed in a given period of time/total size of population) × 100 000

The proportion of *new* individuals in a population diagnosed as having a particular disease in a specific period of time is the *incidence rate*. This is also usually expressed as the number of new cases per 100 000 individuals in the population in that time period, and it is the probability that any single individual in the population will be diagnosed as having the disease in that time period.

Cross sectional surveys can be particularly informative when examining public health issues, as they:

- can be used to determine the prevalence of the disease in the whole population as well as in important sub-groups (eg men and women, risk exposed and non-exposed groups, etc.)

- are useful for examining the effects of factors which do not vary (eg HLA-B27 status and reactive arthritis)
- are generally inexpensive and can be completed (relatively) quickly.

However:

- they have limited usefulness if the disorder is rare or of short duration (since the prevalence will be small and large numbers of individuals will have to be surveyed)
- as exposure and disease are assessed at the same time, it can be difficult to distinguish whether a particular factor is contributing to the aetiology of a disease or is a consequence of having contracted the disease.

Rates

A number of specific rates are used regularly in epidemiological studies.

The **crude rate** for a particular event is the number of occurrences of the event divided by the number of individuals in the population to whom the event could occur eg:

- **Crude attack rate** for an infection: the proportion of people exposed to infection who develop the disease in a given period of time.
- **Crude annual stillbirth rate**: number of still-births (fetuses born dead after 24 weeks gestation) divided by the total number of births, both live and still, in a year.
- **Crude peri-natal mortality rate**: number of still-births and deaths in the first week of life divided by the total number of births .
- **Crude neonatal mortality rate**: number of deaths in the first four weeks of life divided by the number of live births.
- **Crude infant mortality rate**: number of deaths in the first year of life divided by the number of live births.
- **Crude maternal mortality rate**: number of deaths of mothers attributed to pregnancy and delivery divided by the number of births .

- **Crude mortality rate (CMR)** for the entire population of a country for a particular year: total number of deaths occurring in that year divided by the population of the country at the mid-point of the year.

Rates do not have to be restricted to entire populations: **age-specific mortality rate (ASMR)** is number of deaths occurring in an age band of interest divided by the total number of individuals in the population falling into that age band.

Standardised rates

Comparisons between crude rates for different sub-groups can be misleading.

For example, crude death rates in different parts of the country may be influenced by differences in geographical and demographic factors such as age and gender distribution. These can be adjusted for by computing **standardised mortality rates** as follows:

- **Standardised mortality ratio (SMR) for a particular time period**: the ratio of the observed death rate in the study (index) population to the expected death rate

  SMR = (observed deaths in study population/total expected deaths) × 100

- The number of expected deaths is calculated from the age-specific mortality rates in the standard population.
- The population used as the standard population is usually arbitrary and will depend on the purpose of the study.
- SMRs can be calculated for important sub-groups (eg particular communities, occupations, etc.) And may even be used as outcome measures in clinical trials.
- If the SMR is greater than 100 then the mortality rate of that population is increased compared with the standard population.
- If the SMR is smaller than 100 then the mortality rate of that population is decreased compared with the standard population.

11.1.2 Cohort studies

Cohort (longitudinal/follow-up studies) are usually (but not always) conducted *prospectively*. Two groups of individuals are identified from a specific population:

- One group which is currently being exposed to a potential risk factor (*exposed group*).
- The second group which is currently not being exposed to this factor (*non-exposed group*).

Both groups are followed for a pre-determined period of time. The proportions of individuals in each group found to have developed a particular characteristic (usually a disease of interest) are compared (ie the incidence of the characteristic/disease is compared between the two groups).

If there is truly an association, the proportion of individuals with the disease will be higher in the exposed than in the non-exposed group (ie the incidence of the characteristic/disease will be higher in the exposed than in the non-exposed group).

The incidence rates for the two groups are compared by computing a relative risk ratio.

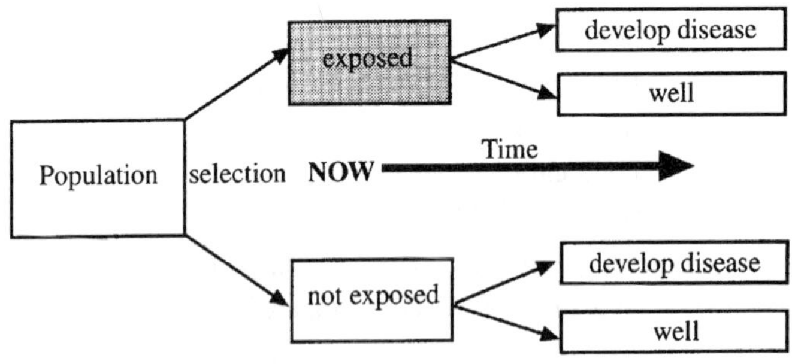

Figure 19 The structure of a cohort study

> **Relative risk ratio**: incidence rate in exposed group/incidence rate in non-exposed group.

If the value of the relative risk is:

- equal to 1: the risks for the exposed and non-exposed populations are identical
- greater than 1: the risk for the exposed group is larger than that for the unexposed group
- less than 1: the risk for the exposed group is smaller than that for the unexposed group.

Relative risks should always be presented with their (95%) confidence intervals:

- The width of the interval indicates the precision of the relative risk estimate.
- If the interval includes 1, the relationship between risk exposure and disease occurrence is *not* statistically significant.
- If the interval does not include 1, the relationship between risk exposure and disease occurrence *is* statistically significant.

> **Attributable risk** (AR): The risk to an individual of developing the characteristic (disease) following exposure to the risk factor (ie the absolute risk that can be attributed to the exposure).
>
> AR = incidence rate in exposed group – incidence rate in non-exposed group
>
> **Population attributable risk** (PAR): The proportion of the risk to the whole population that can be attributed to their combined exposure to the risk factor (ie the (negative) impact of the factor on the entire population).
>
> $$PAR = AR \,.\, (population)\, prevalence\ of\ risk\ factor$$

Cohort studies can be used:

- to measure disease incidence
- to determine the full range of outcomes that can result from exposure to a specific factor (ie they allow the natural history of a disease to be studied)
- to study the effect of exposure to a rare event/factor.

However:

- the effect of only a limited number of exposures can be investigated
- they are not suitable for studying rare disorders/diseases (as it would take too long to accrue the number of occurrences of the disease for the study to have adequate power)
- they tend to be large and expensive, and can take many years to complete
- they tend to be inflexible (a separate study is required to test each new hypothesis).

11.1.3 Case–control studies

Case–control studies are usually (but not always) conducted *retrospectively*. In a sense, they are the reverse of cohort studies. Two groups of individuals are identified from a specific population:

- One group currently has a particular characteristic/disease (*cases*).

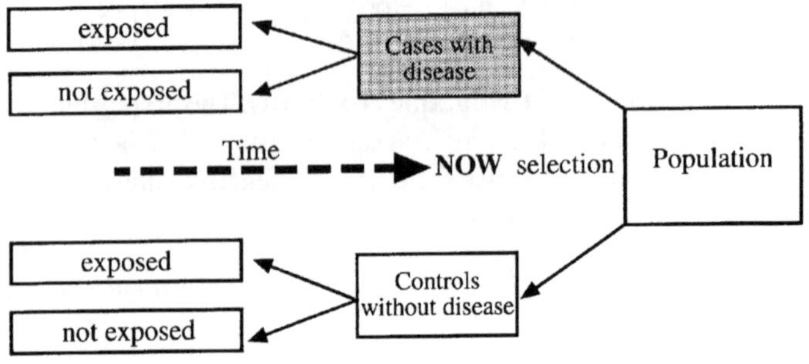

Figure 20 The structure of a case–control study

- The second group does not currently have the characteristic/disease (*controls*).

Previous exposure to a particular (risk) factor is determined in both groups. The proportions of cases and controls exposed to the risk factor are compared (ie the level of risk exposure is compared between the cases and controls).

If there is truly an association, the proportion of cases exposed to the risk factor will be higher than the corresponding proportion of controls. The exposure rates for the cases and controls are compared by computing an **odds ratio**.

Odds ratio: rate of exposure to a risk factor in cases/rate of exposure to risk factor in controls.

If the value of the odds ratio is:

- equal to 1: the likelihood of exposure to the risk factor is identical for both cases and controls
- greater than 1: the likelihood of exposure to the risk factor is greater for the cases than for the controls
- less than 1: the likelihood of exposure to the risk factor is lower for the cases than for the controls.

Odds ratios should always be presented with their (95%) confidence intervals:

- The width of the interval indicates the precision of the odds ratio estimate.
- If the interval includes 1, the relationship between risk exposure and disease occurrence is *not* statistically significant.
- If the interval does not include 1, the relationship between risk exposure and disease occurrence *is* statistically significant.

The choice of controls with this design is absolutely critical. Many different types of control individuals are used, depending on the context of the study, including:

- healthy individuals selected from the general population
- patients with some other unrelated disease

- family members, work colleagues, etc.

Often, control subjects are selected from the list of each case's General Practitioner, as this matches the cases and control by environment/geographical location.

The controls must be similar to the cases with respect to their general characteristics (except, of course, the disease being studied). This is best achieved through careful **matching**, although there are often practical problems associated with this process.

- Matching is carried out during the selection phase of a case–control study.
- Each case is **matched/paired** with one or more control subjects who are as similar as possible to the case for all possible **confounding variables** (ie for all factors that might influence the prevalence of the disease being studied).
- Most case–control studies match for age, gender and geographical location as a minimum. Other confounding factors often matched for include HLA status, blood group and ethnic origin.
- The objective is that, after matching, the cases and controls will differ with respect to just one factor potentially influencing disease prevalence – their exposure to the risk factor(s) being studied.

Case–control studies:

- enable a large number of factors that may be associated with the disease occurrence to be examined
- can be used to study rare diseases
- are generally inexpensive.

However, they:

- enable only one disease to be studied at a time
- are not useful for studying the effects of risk factors that are uncommon/rare
- do not measure incidence.

11.2 Association and causality

ASSOCIATION DOES NOT NECESSARILY IMPLY

The observational study designs outlined in Section 11.1:

- are useful for investigating the potential causes of a disease when a controlled interventional study is not possible
- enable the (statistical) association between a potential causative/risk factor and the incidence of a disease to be appropriately defined and quantified.

However, the results of these studies must be interpreted with caution. The existence of a statistically significant association does not necessarily prove that the link between exposure to a risk factor and the development of the disease is causative.

Three important issues need to be addressed when considering the strength of the argument the association is truly causal.

Type 1 error

As discussed in Chapter 8, Section 8.4, when using a conventional 5% significance test level, a statistically significant result will occur on average once in every 20 tests even though no association exists. This is a type I error. As the number of measures and/or number of sub-groups being evaluated increases, the risk of a type I error also increases.

Statistical methods exist to hold the overall risk of a type I error at a desired level (usually 5%). The most commonly used of these is the **Bonferroni** correction. All effectively require performing each individual statistical test at a much more stringent significance level (eg at 1% or even 0.1%).

Bias

Statistical bias usually occurs because:

- the individuals selected for the study were not adequately representative of the target populations (this usually occurs when non-random samples are selected)
- a poor experimental design was chosen.

As a consequence, there are likely to be factors influencing the measurement of either the disease or the aetiological/risk factors that have not been properly controlled for.

Confounding

Confounding is possibly the most important source of error in observational studies.

This occurs when the exposed and non-exposed groups differ with respect to characteristics that are independent of the risk factor. Such characteristics are called **confounding factors**.

Confounding factors influence the incidence of the disease being studied, but their effects cannot be distinguished from the aetiological/risk factor being investigated.

In other words, confounding factors are associated with the incidence of the disease and so differ between the cases and the controls, but their effects cannot be measured directly.

Example

Early studies of patients with acquired immune deficiency syndrome (AIDS) appeared to demonstrate an excess of amyl nitrate abuse among homosexual males with AIDS relative to those who did not have the disease. Amyl nitrate was thus thought to be a possible cause of AIDS, possibly by some toxic effect on the immune system. Much more is now known about AIDS and the human immunodeficiency virus (HIV). The apparent association observed between HIV and amyl nitrate abuse is now known to have been caused by confounding.

All possible steps must be taken to avoid confounding.

Potential confounding factors can often be identified by referring to previously published studies/literature.

- The effect of confounding factors can sometimes be minimised or eradicated by an appropriate study design (eg if factors such as ethnic origin or gender are possible confounders, the study could be confined to subjects who are male or who are from a single racial group).
- Confounding is much less of a problem in interventional studies. Individuals are assigned to the study groups randomly – if the samples are sufficiently large, the groups obtained should be well balanced with respect to both known and unknown confounding factors.

Having found evidence of a statistical association, is there any external evidence to support the hypothesis that the relationship is causal? To answer the question the following needed to be considered:

- Are the study findings reproducible? Does repeating the experiment, using the same or a different method of examining the same relationship, produce a similar finding?
- Are the study findings consistent? Do similar studies on other populations produce the same findings?
- How strong is the (statistical) relationship between the variables? A small relative risk or odds ratio will be statistically significant if the sample size is sufficiently large, but is the association large (strong) enough to be clinically significant (important)?
- Are there confounding factors that have been ignored or have not yet been identified (ie is the association specific)?
- Is there any evidence of a dose–response? Is the level of risk related to the degree/length of exposure?
- Is the association biologically plausible?
- Is the association reversible? (A strong relationship is known to exist between high blood pressure and stroke, but if hypertension is treated, the risk of developing a stroke is reduced.)
- Does the possibility of reverse causation need to be considered? (In a study of bowel cancer, patients who had carcinoma of the rectum had a high rate of new laxative prescriptions prior to the diagnosis being made. However, the disease was responsible for the high number of laxative prescriptions rather than the alternative conclusion that the laxative used was causing bowel tumours.)

If the above criteria all hold, the observed association is probably a truly causative relationship between the risk factor and the disease. However, this only implies an increased risk – it does not imply that exposure to the factor will inevitably result in an individual developing the disease.

The risk of a young women having CHD is about 1 in 100 000. Using the low-dose oral contraceptive pill possibly doubles this risk. So, when taking the pill, the risk of developing CHD is now about 1 in 50 000. Nevertheless, the risk to any individual woman remains extremely small.

12 Interventional studies/clinical trials

12.1 Rationale for RCT's

Interventional studies have a considerable advantage over observational studies – the investigators have control over who is exposed and who is not exposed to a particular risk factor/intervention.

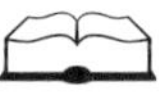

Example

A new drug treatment has been developed for the treatment of ulcerative colitis. Patients with this condition can be (randomly) allocated to receive either the new or the standard drug for four weeks. The proportions of patients healed in the two groups can be compared to determine if the new drug is more effective than the standard drug.

The definitive design for an interventional study is a **randomised controlled clinical trial** (RCT). This design is widely accepted as being the 'gold standard' method for obtaining evidence about the effect of a treatment/intervention.

Interventional studies (including RCTs) must be properly designed if they are to produce valid conclusions. Contrary to popular belief, no amount of statistical manipulation of the results can salvage a badly designed study.

A poorly designed and/or conducted clinical trial is unethical:

- Patients may be exposed to risk (eg a new treatment may have an unsuspected serious side-effect) but the study is unable to produce any clinically useful conclusions.
- The effectiveness of a new treatment may be over-estimated.
- More seriously, the therapeutic advantages of a new treatment might be missed and patients denied access to an effective treatment for their condition.
- Resources will be wasted.

> A good study design is essential.

A properly designed study optimises the chances of accurately estimating the relative effects of the treatments being compared by avoiding potential sources of bias and by controlling for confounding variables.

The efficacy of an intervention (eg a new drug) can only be properly assessed by comparing it against an appropriate control group (eg the standard drug). Thus, RCTs always consist of:

- One or more **treatment groups**, consisting of patients or volunteers who receive the new test treatments/interventions
- One or more **control groups**, consisting of patients receiving no treatment, a placebo treatment or a standard treatment of established efficacy.

> The ethics of using a placebo are complex. In general, a placebo control group is likely to be considered:
>
> - unethical if patients allocated to this group will be denied an established effective treatment
> - ethical if patients will receive the placebo as an adjunct to an established effective treatment.

12.2 Equipoise

In an RCT, patients are not allocated a treatment for their condition on the basis of clinical judgement. Instead, their treatment is selected **randomly** from those being investigated. In this situation, all participating researchers should agree that **equipoise** holds. In simple terms, equipoise exists if there is no definitive evidence suggesting that one of the treatments being compared is better than the others.

In reality, of course, the RCT is usually being carried out because there is reason to believe that the new treatment has therapeutic benefits over the standard treatments. However, at this point, there will be no empirical evidence to support this belief. So, there will be:

- sufficient confidence in the potential effectiveness and safety of the new therapy to justify giving it to the individuals in the *treated* group
- sufficient doubt about the effectiveness of the new treatment to justify not giving it to the *control* group.

12.3 Study protocols

> The study protocol is probably the most important document in a clinical trial.

The study protocol fully details the purpose, design and methodology of the study. Arguably, a new investigator should be able to fully participate in the administration of a study after having read the protocol.

The major components of a good study protocol are outlined in the rest of this section.

12.3.1 Objectives

- The exact objectives (purpose) of the study must be clearly stated.
- Ideally, this should be supported by a brief rationale and literature survey.

- The objectives should be stated in the form of appropriate null and alternative hypotheses.

12.3.2 Design

Uncontrolled clinical trials

- In an uncontrolled clinical trial, all patients receive the same test treatment.
- This design has very limited value, but is sometimes used in preliminary studies to assess tolerable doses, toxicity levels, etc.
- As indicated above, this design does not provide an estimate of treatment efficacy, but may be useful in establishing the *absence* of clinical efficacy or the presence of undesirable adverse reactions.

(Randomised) controlled trials

This design *does* provide an estimate of treatment efficacy. It is used primarily to compare one or more (new) treatments with a control group.

Control groups can take several forms:

- No treatment at all (if this is safe and if spontaneous improvement is likely)
- A placebo (if this is safe, there is no widely accepted standard treatment, and/or a comparison against an inactive treatment is needed)
- A standard treatment (ideally the best of those currently available)

> Two main types of design are used in RCTs.

Group comparative studies

- Each subject is allocated to just one of the treatments (ie the control and treatment groups contain different individuals).
- Between-subject/independent group statistical methods are used to compare the groups.

- Interpretation of the study findings depends on the groups being comparable with respect to important (possibly confounding) characteristics – this is achieved by using robust treatment allocation methods (see below).

Cross-over studies

- Each subject receives several (often all) of the interventions being compared in a randomised sequence.
- Subjects act as their own controls.
- Within-subject/dependent groups/paired statistical methods are used to compare the treatments.

This design is somewhat controversial. It has considerable statistical advantages in that it requires much fewer patients than a group comparative design. However, there is a growing school of thought that cross-over studies are rarely informative.

The problem with this design is the possibility of **carry-over effects**. Adequate time must be left between consecutive treatment periods, otherwise the effect of the first treatment may still be present (partially or wholly) when the second treatment is started. In this case, the two treatment effects are confounded and cannot be separated.

For this reason, the cross-over design:

- requires wash-out periods of adequate length between treatments (so patients may have to be in the study for a considerable period of time)
- requires an assessment of the 'stability of the disease' both before and after the treatments, so may need the use of 'run-in' and 'run-out' periods
- is probably suitable only for treatments with short-term benefits in patients with a chronic but relatively stable disease.

12.3.3 Blinding of assessments

Observer bias can occur in a clinical trial that can seriously compromise the validity of the study findings if:

- either the patient or the clinician (or both) know which treatment the patient is receiving

and/or

- the outcome measures have a subjective element.

Example

A randomised clinical trial is being carried out to compare a new analgesic drug with placebo following wisdom tooth extraction. The analgesic drug, which is being tested at a strong dose, is believed to have sedative effect. One hour after the extraction, the anaesthetist is required to rate the alertness of each patient using an ordinal categorical scale, for which high scores indicate high alertness. Patients often fall between two points on the scale.

When assessing patients known to have been given the analgesic, the anaesthetist may expect to find some reduction in alertness, so may (subconsciously) be biased towards a low rating. But when assessing patients who received the placebo, she may be biased towards a high rating.

At the same time, the patients are required to rate their pain level.

Knowing they were given the analgesic, many patients may be inclined to under-rate their pain, while patients who were given the placebo (and hence not expecting to experience pain relief) may over-rate their pain.

Some of this problem could be avoided by using more objective measures (although, in this context, that might be difficult).

Wherever possible, objective outcome measures should be used in clinical trials. A more effective way of reducing such **observer bias** is to **blind** the patient and/or the clinician to the treatment allocation.

- In a **single-blind study**, the patient (only) has no knowledge of the treatment allocation.
- In a **double-blind study,** neither the patient nor the investigator knows the treatment allocation.
- In a **triple-blind study**, the patient, the investigator and the person analysing the study results are all unaware of the treatment allocation.

(The importance of triple-blindness is often under-rated. If the results of a comparison between two treatments is in the opposite direction to that expected, the results are often checked to ensure they are correct. This is less likely to happen if the difference is in the 'right' direction. Such double standards are unacceptable – and easily avoided by completing the analysis without breaking the treatment code.)

> Blinding studies can be problematic and may require some ingenuity.

Drug treatment comparisons can usually be blinded by using (specially made) versions of the drugs that look (and, ideally, taste) identical.

If this is not possible for some (technical) reason, **double-dummy** methods can be used to good effect. Two identical versions of each drug are used: one version contains the active drug and the other does not (ie is a placebo). Patients allocated to drug A receive the active version of drug A and the placebo version of drug B; patients allocated to drug B receive the placebo version of drug A and the active version of drug B.

In some situations, it may be impractical or unethical for the clinicians running the study not to know the treatment allocation. In this case, an independent assessor can be used, who has no responsibility for the care of the study patients.

> If a study is blinded, a code-break must be easily and readily available at all times in case of emergency (eg a patient takes an overdose of their study medication).

12.3.4 Inclusion/exclusion criteria

The target clinical population (ie the exact nature of the patients to be studied) must be clearly and fully defined. A precise definition of the type(s) of patient (ie exact disease states) eligible for recruitment into the study must be provided in the form of **inclusion and exclusion criteria**:

- These criteria must be comprehensive, covering diagnostic criteria, severity of disease, potential risk factors, length of history, influence of previous/concomitant therapy taken, etc.

- Care is needed to ensure that these criteria do indeed define the most appropriate clinical population for the study. For example, a hospital-based study may not produce findings pertinent to patients attending their general practitioner, and vice-versa.
- The results of a study apply only to the population of patients actually studied and cannot necessarily be generalised to other populations. For example, the results of a trial of a new anaesthetic agent may be difficult to generalise if all the patients included in the study were (young) women undergoing a minor gynaecological procedure (because this was the only type of list the anaesthetist conducting the study was doing during the study period).
- Overly strict and restrictive inclusion/exclusion criteria can result in many potentially eligible patients being excluded – so recruitment into the study will be (dramatically) slower than anticipated.

12.3.5 Interventions/treatments

> The interventions/treatments used in the study must be clearly and fully defined.

Precise but comprehensive descriptions of the interventions/ treatments being compared must be provided, including details of:

- dose, formulation and route of administration
- appropriate mechanisms for increasing, decreasing, or even stopping the allocated treatment altogether where necessary (eg if the study involves dose titration, or if a side-effect is experienced)
- other medication permitted during the study period (eg adjunct or rescue medication)
- the methods to be used to assess the level of compliance for each patient (if appropriate).

12.3.6 Measurements

> The measurements to be used to evaluate the effects of the interventions/treatments must be fully described.

- A **primary outcome measure** should be defined. This is the variable considered to be most important when evaluating the treatments and is used to determine sample size/study power (see Section 12.3.8).
- All other variables recorded are **secondary measures**.
- As far as possible, all measures should be objective, reliable, reproducible and fully validated.

12.3.7 Allocation to treatment

To avoid problems of selection bias, patients must be allocated to the intervention groups using a proper random process. **Selection bias** occurs when the intervention allocated to the next person is known before they have been recruited.

This problem occurs when patients are allocated to the interventions sequentially. In this situation, it is always known in advance which treatment the next patient recruited will receive. If the comparison is between a possible active treatment and a placebo, experience indicates that clinicians are more reluctant to recruit patients into the placebo, even though the active treatment is, as yet, unproved. Consequently, fewer patients are recruited into the placebo group than into the active treatment group. Sequential allocation should *never* be used.

Simple randomisation

- Each eligible patient has an equal chance of being assigned to each intervention group.
- Allocation is determined by random numbers (usually generated by a computer); this is equivalent to tossing a coin or throwing a die.

- Other methods of allocating to treatment, such as using the subject's date of birth or hospital number, may appear random, but rarely are, so should never be used. (Hospital numbers are rarely allocated sequentially, and may have a systematic sequence embedded within them.)

Stratified randomisation

- Ensures that eligible patients with the same potential confounding factors are equally distributed between the study groups.
- Patients are divided into sub-groups (**strata**) defined by the potential confounding factors. Simple random allocation is then carried out within each of the strata separately.
- The proportion of patients recruited into each stratum usually reflects the corresponding population proportions.
- Suppose gender is considered an important confounding factor, requiring stratification. Then separate randomisations will be used for men and women. So, men and women now constitute two strata.

In a study of common cold remedies, we might expect the male and female strata to be equal in size. In a trial of rheumatoid arthritis treatments, we might expect there to be more patients in the female than in the male stratum.

- In some studies, some strata may be naturally very small (eg rare disease sub-groups), in which case, over-recruitment into these strata may be needed to ensure that there are sufficient patients in each strata for statistical analysis.

Example 1
To ensure that two treatment groups were similar with respect to age, patients were divided into the following three age strata, and separate simple randomisation processes used in each:

18–39 years   40–54 years   55–70 years

Example 2
To ensure that two treatment groups were similar with respect to age *and* gender distribution, patients were divided into the following three age strata, and separate simple randomisation processes used in each:

males 18–39 years	males 40–54 years	males 55–70 years
females 18–39 years	females 40–54 years	females 55–70 years

Blocked randomisation

In this method the randomisation process is manipulated to ensure that treatment allocation is equal at fixed points in the recruitment process. For example, randomisation may be blocked in groups of four. So after every fourth patient recruited, the numbers allocated to each intervention group are equal.

Suppose if two treatments A and B are being compared. If the simple randomisation process allocates:

- the first three patients to B, A and A respectively, the fourth patient *must* be allocated to B
- the first two patients to B and B respectively, the third and fourth patients *must* both be allocated to A.

Blocking can be of any size for any number of interventions. However, the block size *must* be a multiple of the number of interventions.

Blocking is done separately within different strata.

The persons recruiting patients into the study should be unaware of the block size, otherwise selection bias problems can occur.

Matching

If all participants in the study are available at its start, **matching** can be used to achieve comparable groups. For a two treatment comparison, subjects who are similar with respect to the important confounding variables (eg gender, age, disease severity) are paired with one another. The members of each pair are then randomly allocated to each treatment.

Matching can, of course, be carried out for any number of interventions.

Minimisation

Minimisation substantially increases the chances of achieving intervention groups that are balanced across important confounding factors.

- A mathematical algorithm is used to determine the extent to which the intervention groups are currently balanced with respect to the confounding measures (imbalance score).

- The next patient recruited is allocated to the intervention group that minimises the imbalance score.
- The calculations are usually sufficiently complex to require the use of a computer program.

12.3.8 Power/sample size

> The optimum **sample size/statistical power** for a study should be determined before the study starts. Not to do so is, arguably, unethical.

- If the sample size is *too small*, a clinically significant difference between the interventions may not be established as statistically significant, in which case, all patients allocated to the experimental treatment may have been exposed to increased risk but no satisfactory scientific conclusions reached.
- If the sample size is *too large*, some of the patients recruited towards the end of the study may have been allocated to an inferior/ineffective treatment unnecessarily.

Lack of attention to power levels can lead to misleading conclusions:

- The early studies of streptokinase on survival following myocardial infarction involved only a few hundred patients and failed to detect any statistically significant effects.
- When larger, more powerful, trials were conducted, a statistically significant increase in survival was detected.
- The increase in survival was small in percentage terms, but clinically extremely important.

The information required to calculate sample size/power is described in Chapter 8, Section 8.6.

Sequential trial design

An alternative to determining the optimal sample size for a study in advance is to use a **sequential design**. After each subject has completed the study, the study observations are assessed to determine whether the current difference between the treatments has achieved statistical significance. The study results are thus continuously monitored until a significant difference is achieved, or until it becomes unlikely (at some defined level) that a clinically significant difference exists.

This approach usually requires fewer patients than when a conventional power calculation is used. However, because of the number of statistical comparisons made, the risk of a type I (false positive) error is increased. This design thus requires the use of complex statistical methods that properly control the overall type I error rate – these are outside the scope of this primer.

12.3.9 Statistical analysis plan

> A general statement of the statistical methods to be used to evaluate the study results should be stated.

The general form of the statistical analysis should be planned before the study starts. The finer points of the analysis may be affected by the observations actually obtained, but not the overall analysis plan. The primary statistical analysis must be restricted to the stated study objectives.

Additional analyses may be indicated by the results of the primary analysis. These should be approached with a healthy mixture of caution and scepticism. The more significance tests that are carried out, the greater the chance of a type I error occurring. Statistically significant results unearthed by 'data dredging' are often not confirmed by later studies.

CONSORT statement

> The **CONSORT statement** is a checklist and flow diagram indicating how the results of a clinical trial should be reported. This statement requires that:
>
> - all patients considered eligible for inclusion in a clinical trial must be accounted for
> - how the sample of study participants to be included in the analysis is determined.

All patients considered eligible for inclusion must be accounted for in the study report. Some patients will be found to violate the inclusion/exclusion criteria and will not be formally included in the study (ie will be excluded). The number of such patients should be reported, along with a summary of the reasons for their exclusion.

All patients randomised into the study must be included appropriately in the statistical analysis. The only exceptions to this rule are patients found retrospectively to be protocol violators.

Three strategies are widely used to determining the sample of study participants to be included in the analysis.

Intention-to-treat (ITT)

ITT is widely regarded as the definitive strategy and the analysis method of choice, as it minimises the possibility of bias due to patients withdrawing or being lost to follow-up. In this strategy, all patients admitted to the study are analysed within the group they were (randomly) allocated to, irrespective the treatment they actually received, their compliance, and whether or not they completed the intervention period. Patients who change (or never even start) their allocated treatment remain, for the purpose of the analysis, in the group they were randomised into.

The ITT strategy generally provides a conservative estimate of the differences between the interventions tested.

Per protocol (PP)

In the PP strategy, only those patients who are considered to have sufficiently complied with the study protocol are considered in the analysis. Compliance usually involves completing all (or a substantial part) of the intervention period and attending for all assessments.

The PP strategy may provide biased estimates of the differences between the interventions as patients who failed to respond and/or experienced intolerable side-effects might be excluded.

Treatment received (TR)

In this strategy, patients are analysed according to the intervention they *actually* received, irrespective of which intervention they were randomly allocated to. This strategy also tends to produce biased estimates of the differences between the interventions.

On occasions, it may be appropriate to use a combination of all three strategies to achieve a complete understanding of the differences between the interventions.

12.3.10 Informed consent

> Participants must knowingly and willingly give their consent to take part in a clinical trial, having first been fully informed of what participation will involve.

Eligible patients must be informed about the study, both verbally and in writing, and then given an appropriate time period in which to consider whether they wish to participate. If they agree to take part, they must indicate their willingness to do so in writing. As part of the consent process, they must be made aware that they can withdraw at any time from the study without having to give a reason and that doing so will not affect either their treatment or their relationship with their clinician.

Informed consent should always be obtained from each patient *before* they are randomised.

12.3.11 Research ethics committees

> All forms of clinical research in the UK involving patients and/or volunteers must be approved by a proper research ethics committee (REC).

A network of RECs has been created throughout the UK to review and approve the ethics of clinical research protocols. No clinical research should be attempted without approval from a REC. The REC network is co-ordinated by an organisation called the Central Office for Research Ethics Committees (COREC). The COREC website contains a huge amount of useful information about the research ethics procedures.

12.3.12 Dissemination of findings

Many grant-awarding bodies now require a detailed account of how the results of a research project will be disseminated before they will offer funding. It is not sufficient to publish the findings in a suitable reputable medical journal. A more extensive strategy is now required, including presentation at appropriate local, national and (where appropriate) international conferences/meetings.

The strategy to be adopted for broadcasting the study findings – and having these introduced into regular clinical practice – must be considered in advance of starting the study.

12.4 Meta-analysis

The number of clinical research papers published in an average year is now immense, and the number is steadily increasing. Many papers report similar studies with apparently conflicting findings. It is becoming impossible for practising clinicians to keep fully aware of the current research findings pertinent to their specialty and to know which research reports to believe!

Meta-analysis are statistical methods that have been developed – and are now in widespread use – to combine the results from similar studies and to extract more accurate estimates of the effects of clinical therapies. By combining the findings of all available studies comparing treatments for particular diseases/conditions using appropriate statistical methods, estimates of treatment efficacy can be obtained with increase power. These methods help to resolve uncertainty in situations where different studies appear to reach conflicting conclusions.

Meta-analyses are particularly useful in situations where there are many relatively small and apparently contradictory research reports and either:

- the results of a definitive randomised controlled trial are not yet available

or

- it would be impractical or unethical to conduct a definitive trial.

The same summary statistics are usually used to indicate efficacy in similar studies, but not always, in which case there may be statistical problems in converting these statistics to a common form before the results can be combined.

For a meta-analysis to be valid, many conditions must hold, including:

- the populations from which the study samples were drawn must be similar
- the designs employed in each study must be similar
- all suitable studies (including any not published) must be included in the calculations.

The final condition is particularly problematic. In addition to the difficulty of identifying relevant studies that, for some reason, have never been formally published (**desk-drawer problem**), there is a problem due to **publication bias**. Positive studies showing differences which are both statistically and clinically significant have a much greater chance of being published than (potentially equally important) negative studies (although some journal editors are becoming aware of this issue and are more amenable to publishing negative findings).

Meta-analyses are co-ordinated and monitored by the Cochrane Collaboration. The website for this organisation contains a wealth of useful information about how to conduct meta-analyses, including a software package for doing the statistical calculations. More importantly, this site also provides access to a huge collection of high-quality meta-analyses spanning all clinical specialties.

13 Outline for critiquing a medical report

Clinical research posts should always be read critically and with an open mind. The absolutely perfect study does not exist – and probably never will. The validity of the study carried out, and hence of the findings reported, should be considered from the point of view of reasonable practice rather than in absolute terms.

Five main questions should be addressed when assessing a report.

1 What question (objective) was the study attempting to answer?

2 What experiment was carried out?
   - (a) Was the type of study carried out appropriate for the study objectives?
   - (b) Was the study population adequately defined and relevant?
   - (c) How were the subjects selected – is there a possibility of selection bias?
   - (d) What control interventions were used – were these appropriate and comparable with the treatment group?
   - (e) Were the study groups proper random samples?
   - (f) Were the study procedures exactly the same for all groups (except for the actual intervention given)?
   - (g) Were the methods and measurements clearly defined?
   - (h) Were there any potential confounding variables that were not considered?
   - (i) Could the assessment methods have introduced (observer) bias – if so, was this adequately dealt with?
   - (j) Do the methods used seem reproducible?

3 What results were obtained?
   - (a) Are the results clearly and appropriately summarised?
   - (b) Do the results make sense and are they consistent?
   - (c) Are the results given in sufficient detail for the reader to reach their own (if necessary different) conclusions?
   - (d) Have appropriate statistical methods been applied, properly reported and interpreted?
   - (e) Have all subjects who were admitted to the study and ran-

domised been accounted for – if the drop-out (attrition) rate was high, does this affect the conclusions that can be drawn?

(f) Have the results been analysed on an intention-to-treat basis?

4 Have the study objectives been met?

(a) Is the result for the primary study objective statistically significant?

(b) Have the summary statistics been presented appropriately (preferably with confidence limits)?

(c) Could the result obtained be explained by other factors than a real difference between the interventions (selection bias, effects of confounding variables, etc.)?

(d) Does the result make sense when compared with findings from previously published studies?

(e) Are the conclusions and findings related directly to the original study objective or are they a consequence of 'data dredging'?

5 Is the result relevant to ordinary clinical practice?

(a) Can the results of the study be generalised (to the sort of population the reader has clinical responsibility for?

(b) Are the results presented in a form relevant to – and understandable to – the likely readership of the report?

14 Sample best of five questions

Mark your answers in the box provided.

1. A group of patients have their albumin levels measured on hospital admission and again 3 weeks into their stay. Which one of the following statistical tests is most appropriate to test the hypothesis that the albumin levels have changed?

☐ **A** McNemar test
☐ **B** Independent samples *t*-test
☐ **C** Linear regression
☐ **D** Wilcoxon's matched-pairs rank sum test
☐ **E** Paired samples *t*-test

2. Admissions to a medical admissions unit were audited for a period of 1 week. For 225 admissions, the mean length of time to see a doctor was 2.5 hours (standard deviation 1.5 h), and the median time to see a doctor was 1.5 h. Which of the following statements is most likely to be correct?

☐ **A** The 95% confidence interval for the mean time to see a doctor is 2.4–2.6 h
☐ **B** Half of all patients waited at least 2.5 h to see a doctor
☐ **C** 95% of patients were seen by a doctor within 5.5 h
☐ **D** The distribution of the times to see a doctor is approximately normal
☐ **E** The distribution of the time to see a doctor is positively skewed

3. In an audit of hospital episode statistics, length of hospital stay for acute medical admissions is found to be highly positively skewed, with a median of 4 days and an interquartile range of 2–10 days. Which of the following statements is correct?

☐ **A** 25% of patients stayed between 2 and 10 days
☐ **B** 50% of patients stayed between 2 and 10 days
☐ **C** 90% of patients stayed between 2 and 10 days

- [ ] **D** 95% of patients stayed between 2 and 10 days
- [ ] **E** All patients stayed between 2 and 10 days

4. In a randomised controlled trial of a new treatment for preventing recurrence of stroke, 1000 patients are randomised to the new treatment and 1000 to standard therapy. A total of 66 patients receiving the new treatment suffered recurrent stroke, compared to 110 in the control arm. What was the relative risk reduction?

- [ ] **A** 4.4%
- [ ] **B** 6.6%
- [ ] **C** 11%
- [ ] **D** 40%
- [ ] **E** 60%

5. After treatment with one of two antihypertensive agents in a randomised controlled trial (involving 50 patients per treatment group), the changes in diastolic blood pressure (DBP) appear to be approximately symmetrically distributed within each treatment group. Which of the following statements is most appropriate for the statistical analysis of the trial data?

- [ ] **A** As the results may not be normally distributed, a non-parametric test for independent samples, such as the Mann–Whitney U-test, should be applied
- [ ] **B** As the results may not be normally distributed, a non-parametric test for paired samples, such as Wilcoxon's matched-pairs rank sum test, should be applied
- [ ] **C** A paired sample *t*-test should be applied to test the null hypothesis that both treatments produce the same mean reduction in DBP
- [ ] **D** An independent sample *t*-test should be applied to test the null hypothesis that the same mean reduction in DBP occurs with each treatment
- [ ] **E** The changes in DBP should be assessed as being of clinical significance or not, and then a chi-squared test used to compare the proportions experiencing a clinically significant improvement in DBP

6. In a large RCT of CBT versus drug therapy in patients with schizophrenia, less than half of the patients completed the study period. Some dropped out by refusing to attend for all of the assessments; some who were allocated to the drug therapy experienced side-effects and so were switched to CBT; some who were allocated to CBT failed to respond and so were given the drug therapy, either with or instead of the CBT. A small group of patients were found to violate the inclusion/exclusion criteria after having been randomised. Which of the following should constitute the primary statistical analysis?

- ☐ **A** All patients randomised, analysed in the groups to which they were originally randomised
- ☐ **B** All eligible patients randomised, analysed in the groups to which they were originally randomised
- ☐ **C** All eligible patients randomised, analysed in the groups in which they completed the study
- ☐ **D** All eligible patients who completed the study, analysed in the groups to which they were originally randomised
- ☐ **E** All eligible patients who completed the study, analysed in the groups in which they completed the study

7. In the first year of an RCT to compare two drugs (A and B) for the secondary prevention of myocardial infarction, there were five deaths in 100 patients treated with drug A and 10 deaths in 100 patients treated with drug B. Which of the following statements is the best summary of the study findings (all of the statistical results quoted are numerically correct)?

- ☐ **A** The uncorrected chi-squared value is 1.802 with 1 degree of freedom ($p = 0.179$), so the treatments are equally effective
- ☐ **B** The Yates (continuity) corrected chi-squared value is 1.153 with 1 degree of freedom ($p = 0.283$), so the treatments are equally effective
- ☐ **C** The Fisher's exact test $p = 0.283$, so the treatments are equally effective
- ☐ **D** The odds ratio for drug A relative to drug B is 0.474 (95% confidence interval 0.156–1.440), so the treatments are equally effective

- E A reduction of 50% or more in the odds of dying in the first year would be considered clinically significant, so the result of this study is equivocal

8. In a crossover trial comparing two drugs to treat children suffering from enuresis, the number of dry nights was recorded in each of two 28-day treatment periods. Which of the following strategies for analysis is likely to be the most appropriate?

- A Construct a contingency table, with the number of dry nights forming the columns and the treatments forming the rows, and apply a chi-squared test
- B For each child, identify the treatment producing the greater number of dry nights, and apply an appropriate test of significance to test the null hypothesis that the proportion of 'preferences' for each treatment is the same
- C Apply a paired *t*-test if the differences in the number of dry nights are approximately symmetrical; otherwise, use a Wilcoxon's matched-pairs rank sum test
- D Apply the non-parametric Mann-Whitney U-test to compare the distribution of the number of dry nights for the two treatments
- E Calculate the correlation coefficient between the number of dry nights on each treatment, and test for a significant correlation

9. Diastolic blood pressure (DBP) measurements naturally follow an approximately normal distribution, with mean 74 mmHg and standard deviation 6 mmHg. Thus, in a random sample of 120 subjects, which of the following statements is most likely to be true?

- A 60 subjects will have DBP levels between 68 mmHg and 80 mmHg
- B There will be six subjects with DBP levels lower than 62 mmHg and six with DBP levels higher than 86 mmHg
- C 23 subjects will have a measured DBP level that is less than 68 mmHg or above 86 mmHg
- D Nobody will have a DBP level of 88 mmHg or higher
- E 40 subjects will have a DBP level above 80 mmHg

10. In a randomised controlled trial of alternative treatments for cystic fibrosis, the primary outcome variable is change in lung function. It is expected that the response will be affected by the severity of the disease, the age of the patient, the centre at which the patient is treated and the baseline level of lung function. In the statistical analysis plan it is most important that:

- ▢ **A** The trial is analysed by an analysis of covariance that incorporates only the variables specified above
- ▢ **B** The trial is analysed by an analysis of covariance that includes all variables that are statistically significant at the 5% level
- ▢ **C** The changes in lung function are analysed using the unpaired Student *t*-test
- ▢ **D** Subgroup analyses are performed for all the variables expected to affect the change in lung function
- ▢ **E** Lung function measurements are standardised for age, sex and height prior to any other analysis

11. An unpaired *t*-test is used to compare the mean post-exercise pulse rates in random samples of patients selected from two different disease populations. The difference in the sample means was 10 beats per minute (bpm) (95% confidence interval –2 to +22 bpm). If a difference of 15 bpm were considered clinically significant, which of the following statements is most correct?

- ▢ **A** We can be 95% confident that there is no difference in post-exercise pulse rate between the two populations
- ▢ **B** There is no real difference in post-exercise pulse rate between the two populations
- ▢ **C** The statistical finding is a type I error
- ▢ **D** The statistical finding is a type II error
- ▢ **E** A non-parametric test should have been used

12. In the design of a randomised controlled trial, to what does the term 'the power of the study' refer?

- ▢ **A** The size of treatment difference that the trial can be expected to detect
- ▢ **B** The probability of rejecting the null hypothesis that the treatments have the same effect
- ▢ **C** The chance that a clinically significant difference will be observed
- ▢ **D** The probability of a type II error
- ▢ **E** The probability of establishing a statistically significant treatment effect if the true treatment difference is at a prespecified level

13. In a prospective clinical trial, 140 patients with hepatitis were randomly allocated either to receive a new drug or to conventional treatment; the patients were followed up for between 3 and 5 years. When evaluating the study results, a chi-squared test can be used to compare the two groups with respect to:

- ▢ **A** The proportions of patients who died within 3 years of starting their treatment
- ▢ **B** The proportions of patients who died within 5 years of starting their treatment
- ▢ **C** The proportions of patients who had died when the study was terminated
- ▢ **D** Median survival times
- ▢ **E** Mean survival times

14. You are deciding on additional treatment for a 22-year-old man who has continuing asthma symptoms on 500 μg/day of inhaled fluticasone dipropionate. When reviewing the available papers on asthma management, which of the following represents the best grade of evidence?

- ▢ **A** A randomised double-blind trial of increased inhaled steroid versus the addition of long-acting beta-agonist therapy
- ▢ **B** An open-label study of increased inhaled steroid therapy
- ▢ **C** A consensus statement from a group of experts

☐ **D** A retrospective analysis of case notes
☐ **E** A prospective observational study

15. In a study to investigate the impact of simple hygiene measures on the rates of MRSA contamination of doctors' tourniquets, a random sample of tourniquets was swabbed before the measures were introduced and a second random sample was tested after the intervention. A reduction in MRSA contamination rates was observed. The result was presented as a 2×2 contingency table with a chi-squared test – the test result was chi-square(1) = 4.8, $p = 0.03$. What does '$p = 0.03$' mean?

☐ **A** 3% of doctors' tourniquets were contaminated with MRSA
☐ **B** If the experiment were to be repeated 100 times, the same result would be found at least three times
☐ **C** The probability that a difference of this magnitude would have occurred by chance is 3%
☐ **D** The probability that this intervention has reduced the contamination rate is 3%
☐ **E** The rate of contamination has been reduced by 3%

16. In an age- and sex-matched case–control study, 20 children with chronic asthma were compared with 20 controls from the same general practice. Their birthweights were compared using a paired *t*-test. This showed that the mean birthweight for the controls was 150 g heavier than for the asthmatics, with a standard error of 100 g. Which of the following is the most appropriate conclusion to draw from this study?

☐ **A** A lower birthweight causes an increased incidence of asthma
☐ **B** Birthweight is not associated with the subsequent development of asthma
☐ **C** There is a statistically significant association ($p < 0.05$) between low birthweight and the development of asthma
☐ **D** There is insufficient evidence to conclude whether or not birthweight affects the development of asthma
☐ **E** The study design is inappropriate

17. Which of the following statements is *not* true for a 95% confidence interval for the difference between two groups?

- ☐ **A** The confidence interval becomes smaller (narrower) as the group sample size increases
- ☐ **B** The confidence interval indicates whether or not the difference between the two groups is statistically significant
- ☐ **C** The smaller (narrower) the confidence interval, the greater the significance of the difference between the groups
- ☐ **D** There is a 95% chance that the true mean difference between the two groups lies inside the confidence interval
- ☐ **E** The confidence interval provides more useful information than the corresponding significance test

18. Researchers have identified 10 clinical symptoms they believe may help to predict how long a person will be off work after suffering whiplash injury in a car accident. Each symptom is assessed separately as 0 = absent, 1 = present. To determine exactly how useful these 10 symptoms are, 200 patients with whiplash injuries were assessed within 7 days of their accident and then followed up until all had returned to work. Which of the following methods is best for analysing the results from this study?

- ☐ **A** Multiple linear regression
- ☐ **B** A series of one-way analyses of variance, with time off work as the outcome (dependent) variable and each symptom in turn as the predictor (independent) variable
- ☐ **C** A paired *t*-test comparing time off work with total symptom score
- ☐ **D** A Pearson's correlation coefficient of total symptom score against time off work
- ☐ **E** A Spearman's correlation coefficient of total symptom score against time off work

19. An oncologist suspects that many women diagnosed as having breast cancer also have high levels of work-related stress. What type of design would be best to test this possible association?

- ☐ **A** Group comparative, randomised controlled trial
- ☐ **B** Crossover, randomised crossover trial
- ☐ **C** Prospective cohort study
- ☐ **D** Retrospective case–control study
- ☐ **E** Prospective observational study

20. A scores obtained by 47 medical students in an MCQ exam were found to correlate significantly with the number of times they practised doing a mock exam (Pearson's $r = 0.307$, $p < 0.01$). Which of the following statements is most likely to be correct?

- ☐ **A** Practising doing mock MCQ exams will ensure a better score in the real exam.
- ☐ **B** For every practice mock exam completed, a student can expect to score 0.307 points higher on average in the real exam
- ☐ **C** For every practice mock exam completed, a student can expect to score 30.7% higher on average in the real exam
- ☐ **D** The number of practice mock exams completed explains less than 10% of the variation found in the real exam marks
- ☐ **E** An r value of 0.307 indicates a very strong mathematical relationship between the number of mock exams practised and real exam performance

Answers

1. **E** Paired samples *t*-test

As the two sets of measurements were made on the same patients at different times they are not statistically independent, so the independent samples t-test (*option B*) cannot be used in this situation. This test is commonly used in error by researchers when analysing paired data: it gives a correct estimate of the change in albumin levels but a totally wrong estimate of its statistical significance.

The remaining tests can all be used legitimately in the situation described.

The McNemar test (*option A*) requires the observations to be reduced to a dichotomy (eg normal/abnormal). This throws away a great deal of useful information. The McNemar test is not optimal for a continuous measure such as albumin level.

Linear regression methods (*option C*) can be used very effectively with paired data, to adjust the values of the second set of observations for the values of the first set (this is often referred to as analysis of covariance). However, this is best reserved for much more complex situations where there are other confounding variables that need to be taken into account, which is not the case here.

The Wilcoxon's matched-pairs rank sum test (*option D*) and the paired samples *t*-test (*option E*) are both valid for this study measure. The choice depends essentially on whether the albumin levels can be assumed to follow an approximately normal distribution. In the absence of any evidence to the contrary, it must be assumed that such an assumption is reasonable and that the use of the more powerful *t*-test is optimal.

2. **E** The distribution of the times to see a doctor is positively skewed

All of the answers could be correct. However, options A, B, C and D all require the assumption that the waiting times follow a normal distribution. Theoretically, times to an event are more likely to follow an exponential distribution. Furthermore, as the mean and median are quite different (2.5 and 1.5 h, respectively), there is empirical evidence that the data are not normally distributed, invalidating *option D*. *Option E* is thus most likely to be true.

Of the remaining options:

- [illegible] interval quoted in *option A* is computed incorrectly. This interval is (approximately) the [illegible]ple mean ± (two standard errors). If the standard deviation is 1.5, the standard error is (1.5/?225) = (1.5/15) = 0.1, so the 95% confidence interval is 2.5 ± 0.2 (ie 2.3–2.7).
- As the data are positively skewed, half the patients will have waited a time equal to or exceeding the median (1.5 h), not the mean (*option B*).
- Again, as the data are not normally distributed we cannot assume that 95% of values lie within two standard deviations of the mean (*option C*).

3. **B** 50% of patients stayed between 2 and 10 days

This is not actually a 'best of five' question as only one of the options can possibly be true. You are being tested here on your knowledge of the interquartile range statistic.

The lower quartile has one-quarter of values below it, and the upper quartile has one-quarter of values above it. The interquartile range, 2–10, is the range from the lower quartile to the upper quartile, so half (50%) of all values lie in this range. Hence, it is *option B* that is correct.

4. **D** 40%

This is also not really a 'best of five' question as only one of the options can possibly be true. You are being tested here on your knowledge of – and ability to calculate – relative risks.

As 66 of the 1000 patients in the new treatment arm suffered recurrent stroke, the risk for this arm was (66/1000) = 6.6%.

The risk of recurrent stroke in the control arm was thus (110/1000) = 11%.

The difference in these risks is the absolute risk reduction: 11% minus 6.6% = 4.4%.

The relative risk reduction is the absolute risk reduction expressed as a percentage of the risk in the control group: 4.4/11 = 40%.

5. **D** An independent sample t-test should be applied to test the null hypothesis that the same mean reduction in diastolic blood pressure occurs with each treatment

Although we are not told that the DBP readings are normally distributed, the independent sample *t*-test is sufficiently robust to be used in the vast majority of cases where the data have an approximate symmetrical distribution. (The normal distribution is, of course, symmetrical.) *Option D* is thus the best option for the situation described.

Of the remaining options:

- The Mann–Whitney U-test (*option A*) would certainly be the first choice if the DBP readings were not symmetrical. This test would also be appropriate if the symmetry was such that the data distribution was very flat or very peaked; there is no evidence that either of these is the case. As non-parametric tests tend to have reduced power, *option A* is unlikely to be optimal here.
- The chi-squared test (*option E*) is a valid method of analysis in this situation but requires the changes in DBP to be reduced to simple dichotomies (clinically significant/clinically insignificant). This would throw away a huge amount of useful statistical information and so is far from being optimal.
- The paired samples *t*-test (*option C*) and the Wilcoxon's matched-pairs rank sum test (*option B*) are both actually invalid, as the study groups are independent (not matched/paired). However, both are used erroneously on many occasions when the numbers of patients in the two treatment groups are equal (giving the impression to the unwary that the observations are matched!).

6. **B** All eligible patients randomised, analysed in the groups to which they were originally randomised

The primary statistical analysis of an RCT should be carried out on an 'intention-to-treat' basis. That is, all eligible patients should be analysed within the group to which they were randomly allocated. This analysis should use all of the data available for all such patients up to and including the point at which they may have been withdrawn from or dropped out of the study. The only patients who might have to be excluded are those for whom only a baseline assessment is available. Thus, *option B* is the optimal primary analysis.

Option A should never be used, as including protocol violators is likely to produce biased and misleading results.

All of the remaining options may provide additional useful information and may have their place in a fully comprehensive analysis of the study findings, but these should [illegible] secondary analyses.

7. **E** A reduction of 50% or more in the odds of dying in the first year would be considered clinically significant, so the result of this study is equivocal

This study failed to establish a statistically significant difference between the treatments, but the observed difference in death rates was large enough to be clinically significant. In essence, the study sample size was insufficient and the study lacked statistical power. The negative result obtained may be a type II error. Thus, *option E* is the best conclusion to draw from this study.

Of the remaining options, the preferred priority order of use would be *option D* followed by *options C, B* and *A*, in that order.

8. **C** Apply a paired *t*-test if the differences in the number of dry nights are approximately symmetrical, otherwise use a Wilcoxon's matched-pairs rank sum test

In a crossover trial such as this the analysis should allow for the possibility of an order (carryover) effect in the data. However, none of the options offered do this, so none is perfect for the situation described.

If it can reasonably be assumed that the effect of the first treatment will not be carried over into the second treatment period, *option C* is optimum, as it advocates the use of an appropriate paired-samples test, with a pre-test for the likely distribution of the differences in dry nights per child.

Options A and *D* ignore the pairing in the observations, so are both inappropriate in this situation.

Option B is a valid method of analysis. However, it requires the observations to be compressed into a simple dichotomy, so is statistically inefficient.

The correlation coefficient suggested in *option E* would indicate whether there was a statistical relationship between the number of dry nights achieved on each treatment, but would not establish whether the average number of dry nights was the same or different between the two treatments.

9. **C** 23 subjects will have a measured DBP level that is less than 68 mmHg or above 86 mmHg

Because of sampling error all of these statements *could* be true, but *option C* is the most likely to be true. This is best demonstrated by considering each option in turn.

Option A. The range 68–80 mmHg is the interval: mean ± 1 standard deviation. For a normal distribution, fractionally over two-thirds of values lie within this interval. So, we would expect to find 80 subjects with DBP readings in this range, rather than the 60 suggested.

Option B. The range 62–86 mmHg is the interval: mean ± 2 standard deviations. For a normal distribution, just over 95% of values lie within this interval. By definition, therefore, just under 5% of values lie outside of this range, with half (2.5%) below the range and half (2.5%) above it. So, we would expect to find three subjects with DBP readings lower than 62 mmHg and three with DBP levels higher than 86 mmHg, rather than the six suggested for both regions.

Option C. 68 mmHg is 1 standard deviation below the mean so, according to the properties of the normal distribution, we would expect approximately one-sixth (= 20) of the subjects to have DBP readings in this region. 86 mmHg is 2 standard deviations, so we would expect to find approximately 2.5% (= 3) of the subjects to have DBP readings in this region. This gives the total of 23 subjects suggested by this option.

Option D. 88 mmHg is 2.33 standard deviations above the mean. According to the properties of the normal distribution, we would expect approximately 1% (= 1) of the subjects to have a DBP reading in this region.

Option E. 80 mmHg is 1 standard deviation above the mean. According to the properties of the normal distribution, we would expect approximately one-sixth (= 20) of the subjects to have a DBP reading in this region, rather than the 40 suggested.

10. **A** The trial is analysed by an analysis of covariance that incorporates only the variables specified above

Option A provides a statistically efficient and unbiased analysis. The final lung function levels are appropriately adjusted for differences in their initial levels. Proper statistical account is taken of all variables considered likely to be influencing the treatment outcomes. Current epidemiological opinion is that this should be done irrespective of whether these covariates are statistically significant or not.

Option B can give results that are misleading. The individual significance levels of the covariates (influencing factors) may be influenced by the other characteristics of the specific sample of patients obtained for the study, and so may not truly reflect the true nature of their influence on treatment outcome (ie they may be *sample specific*). It is therefore better to include them all in the analysis, as suggested in *option A*.

Option C is a valid analysis but a very inefficient test, as it fails to use the information provided by the covariates.

Subgroup analyses should be used sparingly and only with variables expected to modify the treatment effect, so *option D* is not valid.

Standardised lung function measurements can be useful in epidemiological studies, but are unnecessary in a trial where change in lung function is being examined (*option E*).

11. **D** The statistical finding is a type II error

The 95% confidence interval around the mean difference in mean post-exercise pulse rates includes the (null hypothesis) value of zero (0), so the observed difference is not statistically significant. However, the confidence interval also includes values for the mean difference of up to 22 bpm, which are clinically significant. Thus, although the difference is not statistically significant, we cannot exclude the possibility that the true difference is large enough to be considered clinically significant. There is thus a very real possibility that the difference between the populations is clinically important, but this study failed to establish this (ie there is a very real possibility that the statistical finding is a type II error).

Option A looks right, as the 95% confidence interval includes 0. However, all we can say from this interval is that we can be 95% confident that the true population difference is in the region –2 to +22 bpm, which is not the same as the statement made in this option.

Option B is an example of the statistical saw: ‘absence of evidence does not equal evidence of absence’. The observed difference is not statistically significant, but could be real (ie clinically significant), so this statement is false.

A type I error occurs when a statistically significant difference is claimed between two populations when actually no real difference exists. This is not the case here, so *option C* is incorrect.

Finally, there is no evidence in the question that analysing the data with a non-parametric test would be better (*option E*) – although, of course, if the distribution of the pulse rate data was very skewed there might be some virtue in trying this alternative approach.

12. **E** The probability of establishing a statistically significant treatment effect if the true treatment difference is at a pre-specified level

The power of a study is a *probability* statement. It is the probability that, if there is a pre-specified level of difference between the treatment effects, the study will detect this as being statistically significant. The only statement that comes anywhere near this definition is *option E.*

Option A comes close to being correct but fails, as it states that power is the actual size of the difference that needs to be detected, rather than the probability of detecting this size of difference.

Option B also comes close – and, indeed, would be correct if extended to say 'when there is a pre-specified treatment difference'; unfortunately, it is incorrect as it stands.

Option C looks plausible. However, although the pre-specified difference used in a power calculation is *usually* the minimum difference that would be considered to be clinically significant, it does not have to be this value. In some situations (eg exploratory studies or dose-ranging studies), it may be sensible to set this difference higher.

Mathematically, power is the reverse of type II error (ie power = 1 – probability of a type II error), so *option D* is wrong.

13. **A** The proportions of patients who died within 3 years of starting their treatment

Ideally, actuarial (life-table) and/or Cox regression methods should be used to analyse the results of this study, as many of the data collected will be *censored*. These techniques take proper account of the fact that some (possibly the majority) of patients will not reach the study endpoint (death) during the study.

The chi-squared test can be used only to compare categorical measures, so the data must be reduced to this level. The categories usually adopted in this type of study are the simple dichotomy *dead/alive*.

A comparison of the mean and/or median survival times would require the survival times to be retained in their original continuous form, making *options D* and *E* incorrect.

Survival/death rates can only be legitimately compared using a chi-squared test at a fixed point in time following the start of treatment, and all subjects must have been followed up for that length of time. When this study was terminated, patients had been followed up for differing lengths of time, ranging from 3 years to 5 years. *Option C* is thus invalid.

Although all patients had been followed up for at least 3 years, not all had been followed up for 5 years when the study ended. So *option A* is valid, but *option B* is clearly invalid.

14. **A** A randomised double-blind trial of increased inhaled steroid versus the addition of long-acting beta-agonist therapy

Evidence-based medicine uses a system of evidence grading/ranking when evaluating different therapeutic choices.

The highest grade of evidence (the so-called 'gold-standard') is the randomised double-blind controlled trial (RCT) comparing a new treatment against the best alternative therapy (or, in some situations, with placebo). Thus, *option A* is the best answer.

Open-label studies (*option B*) are considered inferior to RCTs. Such studies often have exactly the same design as an RCT, but the results obtained may be biased by virtue of the patients and/or doctors knowing the treatment allocated to each patient.

Next on the ladder of evidence is the observational study (*option E*). Studies may have to use this design if it is impractical or unethical to allocate patients randomly to different treatments, but the evidence obtained is less convincing than from a randomised study. The main problem is that patients will have been allocated to their treatment on the basis of clinical judgement, so the comparisons will be biased.

A retrospective analysis of case records (*option D*) has all the difficulties of interpretation listed for a prospective observational study, with the added difficulty that the data obtained will be of debatable quality. Not all patient notes will have the data required for the study. As the data will have been collected solely for clinical purposes, they may be less accurate than required for a clinical trial.

Finally, expert consensus (*option C*) is considered to be the lowest grade of evidence. Although the views of experts in a particular field are always valuable and should be listened to, these will be possibly based on prejudices and poor knowledge of current research findings, and so may be both biased and outdated.

The Scottish Intercollegiate Guidelines Network (SIGN) group have applied evidence grading to a number of therapy areas, including the management of asthma. The British Thoracic Society/SIGN guidelines represent the best available evidence-based evaluation of asthma management.

15. **C** The probability that a difference of this magnitude would have occurred by chance is 3%

The exact meaning of the statement '$p = 0.03$' is: if the null hypothesis is true (ie the contamination rate was actually exactly the same on both test occasions), the probability that the observed (or a greater) change in contamination rate could have been observed (by chance) is 0.03 (3%). *Option C* is the only statement that agrees with this definition.

Significance test p values indicate the probability of the study data occurring under a specific condition (namely, the null hypothesis). They are not estimates of incidence/prevalence rates. Thus, by definition, *options A* and *E* are totally false.

If the observed finding is a type I error (ie the contamination rates are actually the same, so this study has produced a false-positive result), then *option B* is correct if the significance level for the statistical test is set at 3%. We would indeed expect to obtain a significant test result on average three times out of 100 if the contamination rate remains constant. However, we have absolutely no reason here to believe that the result is a false positive, so this option is unlikely to be true.

The result of this study indicates a very high probability that the intervention has truly reduced the contamination rate. This probability cannot be linked directly to the p value, but is more likely to be nearer to 97% than the 3% suggested by *option D*.

16. **D** There is insufficient evidence to conclude whether or not birthweight affects the development of asthma

The (approximate) 95% confidence interval for the difference in birthweights is mean difference ± two standard errors = $150 \pm (2 \times 100) = 150 \pm 200 = -50$ to $+350$ g. As this interval includes 0 (the null hypothesis value of no difference between the controls and asthmatics), it must be concluded that this study failed to find a statistically significant difference in birthweight between the two groups. Thus, *option C* is clearly incorrect.

Option A is incorrect for the same reason. This statement assumes a statistically significant difference, which is not present. In any case, it is difficult to infer a causal relationship of the type suggested from a simple cross-sectional study of this nature – a longitudinal study would be needed to draw a conclusion of this magnitude.

Option B is a stronger statement than the study result justifies. Certainly, the difference observed is not statistically significant – but a difference of 150 g could be clinically significant. The study sample size is quite small, so there is a very real possibility that this is a type II (false-negative) error. In any case, 'the absence of evidence is not evidence of absence' (see also above).

There is nothing wrong with the observational study design used (except for the inadequate sample size). Indeed, if the only objective was to compare birthweights, this is the only possible design in the circumstances, so *option E* is incorrect. Of course, to establish a causal relationship (if that is the intention) would require the use of either a prospective cohort or a retrospective case–control design.

Thus, the somewhat negative *option D* is the most appropriate conclusion.

17. **C** The smaller (narrower) the confidence interval, the greater the significance of the difference between the groups

Option C is incorrect. In general terms, a narrow confidence interval will *often* indicate a high level of significance between the groups, but this is not always the case. The statistical significance of the difference is determined by the ratio of the mean difference to the standard error of that difference. If both the mean difference and the standard error are small, the 95% confidence interval will be narrow, but the difference may not be statistically significant.

The remaining statements (*options A, B, D* and *E*) are all true.

18. **A** Multiple linear regression

With the single exception of option C (which is invalid), all of these statistical methods would be valid in the situation described.

A paired *t*-test (*option C*) evaluates the change in a single measure (variable) recorded on the same group of individuals on two different occasions. In this instance, two different measures are being analysed, albeit measured on the same individuals, so this option is statistically invalid.

Options D and *E* use the total symptom score (the total number of symptoms present) as a (single) potential predictor of time off work.

Computing this total score assumes that each symptom is equally important and has the same influence on time taken off work, in which case a Pearson's correlation (*option D*) would be valid if either the total score or time off work can be assumed to follow a normal distribution – but if both measures are non-normal, Spearman's correlation coefficient (*option E*) must be used. However, the assumption of equal weight is simplistic, so these options are both probably suboptimal.

A series of one-way analyses of variance (*option B*) would evaluate the predictive ability of each symptom separately, so is arguably better than using the total scores. However, this is a piecemeal analysis that does not readily indicate the relative importance of each symptom. Symptoms with the highest level of statistical significance are probably most predictive. However, this analysis does not indicate whether the symptoms are independently predictive (ie do they provide different information in determining time taken off work?), nor does it indicate what weights should be allocated to each symptom.

Option A answers both of these important questions. A multiple regression analysis with time off work as the outcome (dependent) variable and all 10 symptoms used simultaneously as predictor (independent) variables will determine which of the symptoms significantly – and, importantly, independently – predicts time off work. The standardised regression coefficients will also provide estimates of the relative weight of each symptom in predicting time off work. For example, if the regression coefficient for symptom X is double that of the corresponding coefficient for symptom Y, the weights allocated to symptoms X and Y when calculating total scores should reflect this.

Of course, simple multiple linear regression will be valid only if all patients are followed up until they returned to work. Otherwise, more complex methods, such as Cox regression, developed specifically for the analysis of times to an event occurring, would have to be used. These would allow the study to be terminated early if some patients had not returned to work when the study had to end (eg had a very severe injury), as they can correctly handle 'censored' data.

19. **D** Retrospective case–control study

In this context, a randomised controlled trial (RCT) of any description (*options A* and *B*) would be wholly inappropriate – and probably unethical, as an RCT would involve randomising women to low- or high-stress jobs and then waiting to see how many developed breast cancer. From a strict scientific viewpoint, this is the best way to establish a causal association – but the ideal is not always practical!

A prospective observational study (*option E*) is a viable design but not really appropriate in this situation. Observational surveys are used primarily to measure a single characteristic of interest in a population. If the objective is to look for (causal) associations between two or more characteristics (as is the case here), a different and better approach is needed.

A prospective cohort study (*option C*) is similar in most respects to a simple prospective observational study. However, an important difference is that the study population is divided at the start of the study into two cohorts – those individuals exposed to the risk factor (ie who are in a high-stress job) and those who are not (ie who are in a low-stress job). Both cohorts are followed up for an appropriate period and the incidence of the outcome of interest (in this case breast cancer) is compared between the two groups. Unfortunately, this design has two major disadvantages: it would take a considerable length of time to complete (probably in excess of 10 years in this case) and would involve huge numbers of women (as the incidence of breast cancer is small).

In practice, a retrospective case–control study (*option D*) is optimal. Women who have experienced the outcome (ie have been diagnosed as having breast cancer) are identified and designated as being 'cases'. Each case is matched with at least one woman of the same age and demographic characteristics who has not experienced the outcome (ie has not been diagnosed as having breast cancer): these women are designated 'controls'. The proportions of cases and controls exposed to the risk factor (ie who have a high-stress job) are compared. This design requires a relatively small number of participants and can be completed within a short time, but it does require retrospective recall of important data by the participants. Nevertheless, it is probably the best option for this study.

20. **D** The number of practice mock exams completed explains less than 10% of the variation found in the real exam marks

Options B and *C* are both totally incorrect. Pearson's correlation coefficients measure the strength of the (linear) relationship between two measures. They do *not* indicate the nature of this relationship: this is provided by carrying out a linear regression analysis and examining the regression slope coefficient. There is a mathematical relationship between *r* and the regression slope, but they provide different information. So *options B* or *C* might be true if the regression slope was given, but are definitely not true for the correlation value.

Option A assumes that the statistically correlation found is causal. This may be true – but equally there may be some other explanation. For example, more able and enthusiastic students may be more inclined to practise exam technique, so these students might have obtained higher scores in the real exam anyway. To establish the causal relationship suggested by this option, a more sophisticated study design is needed.

Options D and *E* need to be considered together. The square of the correlation coefficient ($R^2 = 0.307^2 = 0.094 = 9.4\%$) indicates that 9.4% of the variation in real exam scores is explained by the mathematical relationship found with the number of mock exams practised. This means that 90.6% of the variation is unexplained. Viewed in this way, it is difficult to argue that a value of $r = 0.307$ is a *strong* correlation, so the validity of *option E* is extremely debatable.

Index

a posteriori probabilities 14-15
a priori probabilities 14
accuracy 12
actuarial method 93
age-specific mortality rate (ASMR) 99
AIDS 106
alternative hypothesis 60
amyl nitrate abuse 106
analysis of variance (ANOVA) 77-8
annual stillbirth rate 98
ANOVA (analysis of variance) 77-8
arithmetic mean 36
association 105-7
  see also measures of association
attack rates 98
attributable risk (AR) 101
average deviation 38

bar charts 45
Bernoulli variable 92
between-individuals variation 5-6
bias 105-6
  observer bias 112-13
  publication bias 124
  sampling bias 8
  selection bias 116
bimodal frequency distribution 30, 31
binary variables 20-2, 92
binomial distribution 20-2, 67-8
  confidence intervals 57-8
binomial test 66
blinding studies 112-14
blood glucose levels 73-81
blood pressure readings 4-7
Bonferroni correction 105
box-and-whisker plots 48-9

carry-over effects 112
case-control studies 102-4
categorical data 33-5
causal relationships 82-3, 86, 105-7
censored observations 93
centiles 42
central tendency 36-8
chi-squared (χ^2) test 68-9
clinical significance 63
clinical trials
  critiquing a medical report 125-6
  design 108-9
    cross-over studies 112
    group comparative studies 111-12
    randomised controlled trials 111
    uncontrolled clinical trials 111
  equipoise 110
  meta-analysis 123-4
  study protocols 110
    allocation to treatment 116-19
    blinding of assessments 112-14
    blocked randomisation 118
    CONSORT statement 120-1
    inclusion/exclusion criteria 114-15
    informed consent 122
    intention-to-treat (ITT) 121
    interventions/treatments 115
    matching 118
    measurements 116
    minimisation 118-19
    objectives 110-11
    per protocol (PP) 121
    research ethics committees (REC) 122
    sample size/statistical power 119-20
    simple randomisation 116-17
    statistical analysis plan 120-2
    stratified randomisation 117-18
    treatment received (TR) 121-2
Cochran Q-test 70
coefficient of variation 41
cohort studies 100-2
confidence intervals 50-1
  advantages over significance tests 79-81
  binomial distribution (qualitative data) 57-8
  correlations 89-90
  Normal distribution (quantitative data) 54-7

reference ranges 58
standard errors
qualitative data 53
quantitative data 51-3
confounding factors 8, 104, 106
consent 122
CONSORT statement 120-1
contingency tables 68-9
continuous/interval scale 11
control groups 102-4, 109
correlation coefficients 83-6
complex non-linear relationships 88-9
confidence limits/significance tests for correlations 89-90
Pearson correlation coefficient 87, 88, 89
Spearman correlation coefficient 87-8
Cox regression 93-4
critical level 61
cross-over studies 112
cross-sectional surveys 96-100
crude rates 98-9

data
qualitative measures
confidence intervals 57-8
descriptive statistics 33-5
dichotomous and polychotomous 15
graphical presentation 44-5
nominal categorical measures 10
ordinal categorical measures 11
significance tests *see* significance tests
standard errors 53
quantitative measures 11-12
coefficient of variation 41
confidence intervals 54-7
descriptive statistics 35-6
effect size 43
graphical presentation 45-9
measures of central tendency 36-8
measures of dispersion (variation) 38-41
quantiles 41-2
significance tests *see* significance tests
standard deviation 40
standard errors 40-1, 51-3
variance 39-40

death rates 98-100
degrees of freedom 69
dependent variable 83
descriptive statistics
importance 32
qualitative/categorical data 33-5
quantitative data 35-6
coefficient of variation 41
effect size 43
measures of central tendency 36-8
measures of dispersion (variation) 38-41
quantiles 41-2
standard deviation 40
standard error 40-1
variance 39-40
desk-drawer problem 124
deviates 38
diastolic blood pressure (DBP) readings 4-7
dichotomous measures 15
discrete continuous measures 11-12
dispersion 38-41
distributions 20
binomial distribution 20-2, 67-8
confidence intervals 57-8
log-Normal (continuous) distributions 29
non-Normal (continuous) distributions 27-9
measures of dispersion (variation) 41
Normal (Gaussian) distribution 23-5
confidence intervals 54-7
measures of dispersion (variation) 38-41
standard Normal distribution 26
normalising transformations 29-31
Poisson distribution 23, 30
Student t-distribution 27, 55-7
dependent samples/paired t-test 76, 77
independent samples/unpaired t-test 74-6, 77
one-sample t-test 74
dot diagrams 45, 46
double-blind studies 113
double-dummy methods 114

effect size 43

epidemiology 95
  observational studies 95-6
    association and causality 105-7
    case-control studies 102-4
    cohort studies 100-2
    cross-sectional (prevalence) surveys 96-99
equipoise 110
errors
  bias 105-6
    observer bias 112-13
    publication bias 124
    sampling bias 8
    selection bias 116
  confounding factors 8, 106
  measurement error 4
  type I 62-3, 105
  type II 62-3
see also standard errors; variation
estimated probability 71-2
estimates 50
ethics 109, 122
evaluation 125-6
exclusion criteria 114-15
expected values 68-9, 72
extrapolation 90

F-statistic 77
false-negative/positive results 19, 62-3
Fisher exact test 67
Fisher z-transformation 89
follow-up studies 100-2
frequency counts 33-4
frequency distributions 47-8
Friedman test 78

Gaussian distribution 23-5
  confidence intervals 54-7
  measures of dispersion (variation) 38-41
  standard Normal distribution 26
geometric mean 36-7
graphical presentation
  qualitative measures 44-5
  quantitative data 45-9
group comparative studies 111-12

hazard rate 94
histograms 46-7
hypotheses 60-2
hypothesis tests *see* significance tests

inadequate power 8
incidence 96, 97
incidence ratios 35
inclusion criteria 114-15
incorrect diagnosis 19
independent variable 83
infant mortality rates 99
informed consent 122
intention-to-treat (ITT) 121
interpolation 90
interquartile range 42
interventional studies *see* clinical trials

Kaplan-Meier method 93
Kappa statistic 70
Kruskal-Wallis test 77

Levene test 75
life-table analysis 93
linear regression 90
  model residuals 92
  multiple linear regression 91
  non-linear relationships 91
log-normal (continuous) distribution 29
log-rank test 94
logistic regression 92-3
longitudinal studies 99-100

Mann-Whitney U-test 75, 77
matching 104, 118
maternal mortality rates 99
McNemar test 70
mean calculations 36-7
measurement error 4
measurements
  accuracy and precision 12
  clinical trials 116
  interventional studies 115
  qualitative
    confidence intervals 57-8
    descriptive statistics 33-5
    dichotomous and polychotomous 15
    graphical presentation 44-5
    nominal categorical measures 10
    ordinal categorical measures 11
    significance tests *see* significance

tests
standard errors 54
quantitative 11-12, 44
coefficient of variation 41
confidence intervals 54-8
descriptive statistics 35-6
graphical presentation 44-9
measures of central tendency 36-8
measures of dispersion (variation) 38-41
quantiles 41-2
significance tests *see* significance tests
standard deviation 40
standard error 40-1, 51-3
variance 39-40
validity 13
measures of association
correlation 83-6
complex non-linear relationships 88-9
confidence limits/significance tests for correlations 89-90
Pearson correlation coefficient 87, 88, 89
Spearman correlation coefficient 87-8
Cox regression 93-4
linear regression 90
model residuals 92
multiple linear regression 91
non-linear relationships 91
logistic regression 92-3
scatterplots 82-3
survival curves 93-4
median 37, 42
meta-analysis 123-4
MICA study 96
minimisation 118-19
missed diagnoses 19
mode 37-8
mortality rates 98-100
multiple comparison tests 77

natural variation 5
negative correlation 84
negative predictive value 18-19
negatively skewed distribution 28-9, 31
neonatal mortality rates 98
nominal categorical measures 10
non-Normal (continuous) distributions 27-9
measures of dispersion (variation) 41
non-parametric tests 72-3
Normal (Gaussian) distribution 23-5
confidence intervals 54-7
measures of dispersion (variation) 38-41
standard Normal distribution 26
normalising transformations 29-31
null hypothesis 60-2
number needed to treat (NNT) 71-72

observational studies 95-6
association and causality 105-7
case-control studies 102-4
cohort studies 99-102
cross-sectional (prevalence) surveys 96-99
observed values 68
observer bias 112-13
odds ratios 35, 92-3, 103
one-way analysis of variance (one-way ANOVA) 77-8
ordinal categorical measures 11
outcome variable 83, 92, 116

p-values 60-2
parametric tests 73
Pearson correlation coefficient 87, 88, 89
per protocol (PP) strategy 121
percentage agreement 70
percentages 33-4
percentiles 42
perinatal mortality rates 98
pie diagrams 44
placebo 109, 113, 114
Poisson distribution 23, 30
polychotomous measures 15
population attributable risk (PAR) 101
populations 2-4
positive correlation 84, 85
positive predictive value 18-19
positively skewed distribution 28-9, 30-1
precision 12
predicted variable 83
predictor variable 83
prevalence surveys 96-99

primary outcome measure 116
probability
  definitions 14-15
  independent events 17
  mutually exclusive categories 16
  properties and notation 15-16
  sensitivity and specificity 17-19
probability distribution 22
publication bias 124

qualitative measures
  confidence intervals 57-8
  descriptive statistics 33-5
  dichotomous and polychotomous 15
  graphical presentation 44-5
  nominal categorical measures 10
  ordinal categorical measures 11
  significance tests *see* significance tests
  standard errors 52
quantiles 41-2
quantitative measures 11-12
  coefficient of variation 41
  confidence intervals 54-7
  descriptive statistics 35-6
  graphical presentation 44-9
  measures of central tendency 36-8
  measures of dispersion 38-41
  quantiles 41-2
  significance tests *see* significance tests
  standard deviation 40
  standard errors 40-1, 51-3
  variance 39-40
quartiles 42

random samples 3
random sampling variation 7
random variation 6
randomisation 116-18
randomised clinical trials (RCTs) *see* clinical trials
reference ranges 58
relative frequency distribution 47
relative incidence ratios 35
relative risk ratio 100-1
repeated measures analysis of variance (ANOVA) 77
replicates 5, 12
representative sample 3
research ethics committees (REC) 122
research evaluation 125-6
residuals 92
responsc variable 83
risk difference 71, 72
risk exposure 100-1, 102-3

sample size
  confidence intervals 54-8
  statistical power 64-5, 119-20
sample variation/error 6-7
samples 2-4
sampling bias 8
sampling distribution 52
scatterplots 82-3
secondary measures 116
selection bias 116
SEM (standard error of the sample mean) 52-3
sensitivity 17-19
sequential trial design 119-20
significance level 61
significance tests 59-60
  advantages of confidence intervals over significance tests 79-81
  clinical vs statistical significance 63
  correlations 89-90
  hypotheses 60
  qualitative data
    dependent samples 70
    number needed to treat 71-2
    single sample 66
    two or more independent samples 67
    worked example 71-2
  quantitative (continuous) data
    more than two samples 77-8
    parametric and non-parametric methods 73
    single samples 74
    two dependent samples 76-7
    two independent samples 74-6
  sample size and statistical power 64-5
  test statistics 61, 65-6
  type I and type II errors 62-3
simple random sample 3
single-blind studies 113
skewed distribution 27-9
Spearman correlation coefficient 87-8
specificity 17-19
square of the correlation coefficient 86

MONKLANDS HOSPITAL
LIBRARY
MONKSCOURT AVENUE
AIRDRIE ML60JS
☎01236712005

standard deviation 40
standard errors 40-1
  qualitative data 53
  quantitative data 51-3
  SEM (standard error of the sample mean) 52-3
standard Normal distribution 26
standardised mean difference 43
standardised mortality ratio (SMR) 99
statistical analysis plan 120-2
statistical power 64-5, 119
statistical significance 61-2, 63
statistics
  definition and use 1-2
  importance 32
  qualitative/categorical data 33-5
  quantitative data 35-6
    coefficient of variation 41
    effect size 43
    measures of central tendency 36-8
    measures of dispersion (variation) 38-41
    quantiles 41-2
    standard deviation 40
    standard error 40-1
    variance 39-40
stillbirth rates 98
stratified randomisation 3, 117-18
Student t-distribution 27, 55-7
  dependent samples/paired t-test 76, 77
  independent samples/unpaired t-test 74-6, 77
  one sample t-test 74
study design 8-9, 108-9
  cross-over studies 112
  group comparative studies 111-12
  uncontrolled clinical trials 111
study evaluation 125-6
study population 2
study protocols 110
  allocation to treatment 116-19
  blinding of assessments 112-14
  blocked randomisation 118
  CONSORT statement 120-1
  inclusion/exclusion criteria 114-15
  informed consent 122
  intention-to-treat (ITT) 121
  interventions/treatments 115
  matching 118
  measurements 116
  minimisation 118-19
  objectives 110-11
  per-protocol (PP) 121
  randomised controlled trials 111
  research ethics committees (REC) 122
  sample size/statistical power 119-20
  simple randomisation 116-17
  statistical analysis plan 120-2
  stratified randomisation 117-18
  treatment received (TR) 121-2
sum of squares 39
survival curves 93-4
systematic variation 5-6

t-test *see* Student t-distribution
target population 2
test statistics 61, 65-6
transformations 29-31
treatment groups 109
treatment received (TR) 121-2
triple-blind studies 113
type I errors 62-3, 105
type II errors 62-3

uncertainty 1-2
uncontrolled clinical trials 111
unimodal frequency distribution 27
unknown/unobserved variation 7

validity 13
variance 39-40
variation 1-2, 38-41
  between-individuals variation 5-6
measurement error 4
sample variation/error 6-7
systematic effects 5-6
unknown/unobserved variation 7
within-individual (natural) variation 5

Wilcoxon matched pairs rank-sum test 76, 77
within-individual variation 5